DOG
TRAINING
AND
BEHAVIOUR

DOG
TRAINING
AND
BEHAVIOUR

UNDERSTANDING YOUR DOG'S MIND

JOHN CREE

SWAN·HILL
PRESS

First published in the UK in 2006
by Swan Hill Press, an imprint of Quiller Publishing Ltd

British Library Cataloguing-in-Publication Data
   A catalogue record for this book
   is available from the British Library

ISBN 1 904057 85 3
    978 1 904057 85 7

Printed in England by Cromwell Pres Ltd., Trowbridge

Swan Hill Press

An imprint of Quiller Publishing Ltd
Wykey House, Wykey, Shrewsbury, SY4 1JA
Tel: 01939 261616 Fax: 01939 261606
E-mail: info@quillerbooks.com
Website: www.countrybooksdirect.com

DEDICATION

To the dogs, my own German Shepherds and all the
others, who have come into my life throughout the years.
They have been such good company.

ACKNOWLEDGEMENTS

Quite a number of dog owners in both domestic and competitive fields have unconsciously, over the years, helped me prove and improve many of my theories that eventually became standard practices. Without that knowledge, there would have been little material for this project.

In preparation for this publication, a number of owners have given their time and concentration while I took the photographs that were so necessary to ensure that the readers had the opportunity to benefit from the matching up of the visual and the written word.

I give thanks to these owners who are: Pam Cuthbert with Milo, Frances Ball with Alice, Colin Ball with Tucker, Ruth McGuigan with Jaspser, Joyce Rae with her puppy Travis, Doreen Bidgood with a few of her boarders at Quarrybrae Kennels.

I must also thank Irene, my wife, for ensuring that the text could be read with the intended meaning.

CONTENTS

INTRODUCTION

There are many books on the market that cover various aspects of dog training and behaviour problems and some are very good. I have written some myself. However, we can write what we think is right with full instructions on what to do and how to do it, possibly with a touch of philosophy thrown in, if it is recognised as such. However, is it enough to create a full understanding of the subject? Whatever the source or extent of your knowledge on training, the degree of your success is likely to be determined by an understanding of the principles behind the activity – the philosophy of dog training

For the individual owner, trainer or instructor, they should understand themselves, the dogs and the training routines, then recognise the need for both a practical and a theoretical background. This can only make the function easier and more pleasurable for all concerned. With this additional knowledge and ability, less can go wrong. There will also be a greater understanding of any problems that may arise during training or behaviour management.

Notes:
1. For convenience, I shall make use of the male gender unless the subjects relate particularly to the female sex.

2. Although it is common practice in dog clubs within the UK to refer to the dog owner as the 'handler' and the instructor as the 'trainer', in some professional situations, trainers actually train the dogs, and then the dogs are given to a handler for operational purposes. In those situations, the person working the dog would be the handler. However, to avoid confusion in these writings the owner will be defined as such, or 'you' may be used as an alternative to define the party who is actually training the dog.

PREFACE

The content of this book is directed at any interested party who is involved in training a dog. It may be the pet dog owner who wants to have the enjoyable companionship of a canine friend who is happy to accept the training that will ensure he will fit in with a controlled domestic environment. On the other hand, the dog may also be used for competitive or operational purposes. All situations are built on a similar basis. The philosophy does not change, only the magnitude of application changes as the objectives become more complex and demanding. The dogs have to learn more and the complexity of the tasks also requires greater knowledge from the person training the dog.

In all these situations, there are objectives that require the trainer (and subsequently known as 'you' or the 'owner') to take the initiative required when applying strict control. There are other occasions when the dog knows, through training, what is expected of him without the demands of authority. There are still other situations where the owner eventually becomes the junior partner, giving the dog the opportunity to apply his initiative within the scope of the objective.

The knowledge imparted in these pages come from the best part of fifty years of dog ownership and involvement to the training for good companionship along with the fields of Obedience competitions and Working trials. This includes almost as many years of instructing, counselling and assessing the performance of others.

Training and behaviour management may be considered by some to be two separate subjects, but in the main, they have the same foundation for control and the development of conditioning to solve and overcome a behaviour problem. When I discuss the principals within the various aspects of training, the conditioning within the field of behaviour management should also be included.

PART 1

Chapter 1

A Background to Training

Dog training is a form of education where firstly, by means of books on this subject, by attending training classes or courses, owners are educated on how to train their dogs. It is only when the owner has a grasp of the subject that dog training can progress.

As novice owners are themselves learning while they teach their dogs, it will be seen that many dogs receive their education second hand. Every transfer of information, from book to instructor, on to owner and then to the dog, is likely to cause a misinterpretation of the orignal intention. With the dog at the end of the line, he is most likely to be condemned as the stupid link in the chain, may well be blamed for the failures which originate from its source, the book, instructor, or from the owner.

Iceni training session for all breeeds.

We, as human beings, require an incentive or inducement to learn. Children at school, students at college, or adults at work, are all being educated or trained in a particular skill. If the incentive is strong enough, or if the goal is well worth achieving, we shall work hard enough for it. The subject will attract and keep our interest and any obstacles will be overcome because we appreciate the value of success; we shall also realise the meaning of failure. Fear, as an inducement to work, can affect humans and dogs in a simlilar manner. Attention is split between the subject being taught and the cause of the fear. There is no doubt that dogs can be and are trained through fear of their owner or the instructor, but it does show a lack of ability to achieve the objective by more constructive and considerate means.

Fortunately, as humans, we can visualise the end product and will work for it. With dogs the end product is much more immediate (an intermediate stage) and, if they cannot visualise the end product, they will go their own way. A dog will normally act in a manner which he thinks is in his best interest.

Your dog is one of the family, a companion and a source of enjoyment, but he can also be an embarrassment, infuriating at times and can cause some displeasure to yourself, your neighbours or complete strangers by the unpleasant situations that can develop through his activities. This is the family dog – our domestic canine companion.

His companionship and the pleasure he gives must outweigh any periodic irritations caused by wayward activities, so that he can remain a welcome member of the household, but is this sufficient? Any misdemeanours may be small and infrequent and this may well be due to the owner's own understanding and ability. On the other hand owners may not have such a natural gift of understanding their companion's requirements and may well find their dog's companionship rather trying at times.

In many ways we can liken dogs with children, children can be as embarrassing, infuriating and the source of as much displeasure as any dog. There is so much experience in the world of bringing up children, of educating them to become independent and responsible and yet, there are so many mistakes or misjudgments that we find ourselves in such an imperfect world. No wonder there are problems with domestic pets, when canine psychology is a specialised subject. If he is also being trained for competitive work or a more professional function, behaviour or constructive training can be hampered by the same embarrassing situations.

Dog training should always be considered as a pleasurable experience for both dog and owner. Yes, there will be times when undesirable situations require less pleasurable activities for both dog and owner. A short and temporary application of a strict and demanding method can be justified as a small consideration to achieve the desired result, if the end product is that of enjoyment for both dog and owner.

Dogs enjoy the end result when a training programme is executed with consideration for his capability to co-operate, and this will induce his owner to continue with the dog's well being in mind. From the humble domestic pet dog to the highly trained professional and the training for simple day-to-day actions to the complex scenting or protection activities, this will create a more highly active brain that will give lasting pleasure and pride for their accomplishments.

Although some domestic dog owners have had no difficulties in achieving control over their canine friends it is not necessarily due to a knowledge of the subject. It is possibly due to a natural ability, a most precious gift, and having a dog that wants to please. We should all envy such a partnership, but may not learn much from it.

Understanding the dogs themselves may not be easy, and I believe that understanding ourselves, as dog owners, can also have its difficulties. There is often the case of thinking of human actions when an owner should be giving consideration to the canine thought process. The dog's mental process governs his responses, satisfactory or otherwise. We must also consider what gives a dog satisfaction, or why he can be reluctant to co-operate.

Some owners have a few natural skills, perhaps sufficient for domestic situations, and as a starting point for the development into the more serious aspect of competitive and professional field of work. There are however, people who seem to be completely devoid of any of the skills required for dog training. I always think of my experience with two of my clients who were both members of the medical profession; one was a general practitioner and the other was a highly skilled orthopaedic surgeon, both attended my group domestic training classes. The GP with his Springer Spaniel had a great natural ability to understand my instructions and to carry them out in the most appropriate manner. He could use his hands, arms, body movement and his voice with the variations that controlled each of his dog's responses. It was a joy to watch man and dog responding to each change in situation, and to the pleasure they both got from it.

The surgeon was a complete disaster. I could tell him, show him and demonstrate to let him see that his Labrador could be more than co-operative. When I had the dog on the lead and carried out my attention generating routine, all the surgeon could say was 'you hypnotise that dog'. Eventually he gave up and let his fourteen-year-old daughter bring the dog for training. The situation changed completely and the Labrador responded beautifully to the natural skills of this young girl.

It is so easy to criticise individuals for their inability to handle canine situations. However, we all have our own levels of natural aptitude and ability to understand how to deploy our timing, movements and vocal inducements to cope with a dog that may have his own deficiencies. All people are different and all dogs have their varying strengths and weaknesses and this makes every dog/owner partnership unique. Although standard training practices have a very strong place within our field, their applications have to be geared towards the individual partnerships.

Chapter 2

UNDERSTANDING DOGS

Introduction

The social behaviour and the ease or difficulty owners have in achieving the requirements for the domestic scene are greatly affected by the choice of their canine companion. Some dogs are much more responsive than others. Some dogs fall into the pattern of home life without the need to consider any formal methods of training. In cases like this it is usually found that dog and owner have been matched to perfection. This is where the dog has inherited a very balanced character whilst the owner, by design or accident, has the knowledge and ability to prevent unsociable activities from developing. However, these combinations rarely seem to be fully matched.

It must be recognised from the start that no two dogs have the same character, temperament, or inherited instincts and even within a single litter of puppies there are variations. Some puppies are bold and brash whilst others are shy and retiring. Some puppies are very quick witted and will size up situations as they are developing, while others do not seem to notice such changing conditions.

The various working qualities that have been bred into, or out of different breeds will add another factor to the composition of each dog, gundogs will show quite a different set of characteristics from those of the terrier families, even within the gundog group each breed has been developed for its own special contribution to the sport. The difference between one dog and another can be experienced in so many different ways, some dogs can be naturally attentive whilst others can show quite a streak of independence.

Some are very attached to their own kind whilst others prefer human companionship. Some dogs are very energetic and enjoy plenty of space to run free while others have a much more contented outlook on life. Some dogs are very inquisitive and will stop to investigate anything that takes their fancy, while others can seem to spend their time daydreaming. Some dogs are very protective and will warn off any stranger while others show no sense of discrimination; they will even welcome burglars into their homes. However, all dogs will have a certain mixture of all these characteristics bred into their systems and in such a varying strengths that each dog can be considered as a unique canine creature.

It should also be recognised that each dog has its own age of reaching mental maturity. Some small breeds seem to mature, both mentally and physically, at an early age. Labradors, Dobermans, German Shepherds and such like require much more time to settle down before they can be ready for advanced training. This age to maturity may also affect the time any youngster takes to settle into a sociable domestic existence and any dog owner should give due consideration to his dog's natural inherited characteristics before making an excuse for any undesirable situation he himself may generate.

The same thinking can be extended to cross breeds and mongrels, as they will inherit their characteristics through their parents. This may result in some excellent combinations and produce youngsters of very sound character and temperament, on the other hand combinations of genetics that make up this inheritance can result in dogs which require a great deal of understanding.

We must not forget the breeder, because the early environment will have a bearing on the future. This is especially true when a pup goes into a new home too early in his life or the pick of the litter has lead a sheltered life and is finally discarded and at a high price when its future in the show ring does not come up to expectation.

From the beginning

It is now fully recognised that all breeds of dogs have developed from the wolf through the ages, no doubt with a touch of coyote and jackal thrown in. The principal characteristic that connects dogs with these animals is the number of chromosomes ($2n=78$) is the same for each one – they can inter-breed.

Some breeds of dogs are very much closer to the wolf than others. The Eskimos in Canada cross wolves with their sledge dogs to improve the stamina of the next generation. It may be difficult to think of some of our small breeds originating from the wolf, but there are different types of wolves throughout the world and not forgetting the effect of coyotes and jackals. Over the centuries, man has manipulated the breeding of animals to suit his own ends. I would think that any animal, be it domestic or farming livestock has changed in looks, size and character from the original species in the wild.

With a number of breeds, shepherding is the principle characteristic that has been manipulated to give us highly successful breeds for the purpose of animal husbandry. Hounds and gundogs have been developed to give food on the table and the guarding breeds for the defence of families, communes and the livestock associated with early human life. So many of these animals were also the foundation of some breeds that do not seem to have an ounce of working ability and were developed to suit the particular fancy of a pure domestic environment.

Each dog today has inherited and contains, at least a vestige of its beginnings from the wolf. Hunting and guarding have come through to some extent. Some features have been combined to give us the shepherding breeds that are also known to be excellent as guard dogs. Even the little Chihuahua is known for the defensive stance it can take up.

Perhaps it is time to look at the wolf and its development into a useful domesticated pet. It is also time to look at dogs, our own and others in the community, to visualise the origins of so many of these dogs.

It should be acknowledged that the wolf pack is held together in a hierarchy of *dominance, submission, affection and fear*. A proper pecking order being established with the strongest willed and fittest male or female applying the dominance required to achieve control of, and within, the pack.

Like our present day *canine* friends, each wolf would be unique in character and ability to contribute to the pack's activities. The principal activities would be hunting for food and the protection of its own kind. Although the character of each wolf would be unique it would be within certain defined patterns. Like the human race there would be some wolves born to lead, others born to follow, yet others who would like to lead but are required to submit into an inferior role within the pack.

An important feature of any breed of dog is temperament and it would be difficult to consider the temperament of the wolf of the past within today's assessment of conditions. They may well appear to be nervous or shy near human company and this could be due to their ability to 'accommodate environmental experiences'. Throughout the ages a pack of wolves or a solitary one would go for an easy kill to fill their stomachs. This may be a child or a domesticated animal. The wolf itself may have been on the menu for early man. Wolves had good reason to be cautious of early man and his intentions, why should they wait around to find out?

We all like to think that loyalty from dog to his owner is important and a natural characteristic, but loyalty is something that should be earned and goes both ways. In wolf terms loyalty to the pack and its leader was the foundation of their group system of existence, that of dominance, submission, affection and fear. The dominance of the leader carried the responsibility of managing the pack by applying his/her authority. This authority could only be gained by the ability to lead and ensure that food could be found. If this food were 'on the hoof' then his guile, courage, intelligence and the other lead characteristics would be tested in turning a mobile prey into a welcome meal.

Submission to the leader was vital to achieve reasonable harmony within a pack. It also created respectful affection. The challenge to leadership or the sorting of a pecking order down the line could be disruptive, and no doubt was from time to time.

It is the submissive nature of the majority of wolves to their leader that is probably the most important factor in the domestication of any wolf into the human pack, and it is very doubtful if potential leaders in the wolf pack would have integrated with human society. The ability of so many to submit to a leader certainly helped to make these animals an accepted addition to early human life.

The submissive behaviour of the wolf would depend on the attitude of the more dominant animal, be it wolf or man. A very dominant attitude from the leader would result in a more subordinate and submissive response. If the more masterful authority was too tolerant without showing the appropriate degree of dominance, the subordinate wolf would try to assert himself. If the dominant party were over aggressive in his domination, the subordinate and submissive wolf would be more likely to retreat through fear and could become insecure within the pack. If the situation was bad enough he may find life on the outside of the pack to be more acceptable. Within this paragraph it is easy to equate the dominant human being with his dogs, or even his own family

It was the wolf's power of reasoning and adaptability that helped to achieve survival. Having the ability to take on prey larger than themselves required an intelligent decision and, if need be, the co-operation of the group. Some wolves with better scenting powers would detect a track or wind scent the target and therefore take the lead. Others with good long distance sight could spot movement at a distance and lead the pack to their quarry. The most aggressive and courageous could then make the initial attack and immobilise their prey so that full bellies were assured for the whole pack. The ability of wolves to co-ordinate the strengths of the various individuals was an indication of their capacity in the field of intelligence.

Tackling animals larger than themselves to secure a meal, even in the form of mob violence, took courage. No doubt there would be a number of wolves that would be happy to follow and give moral support. The animals that took the risk of a hoof in the ribs or skull, a slash from a set of antlers or being crushed by a fallen beast had the fearlessness that ensured their position in the hierarchy of the pack.

The vigilant application of all senses would ensure that unwanted visitors were detected. The senses of smell and hearing would be of particular value. Again with the prerequisite of locating their next meal or the presence of unwanted visitors, the alertness of these senses plus that of sight would be essential for their survival.

The tireless dedication to the search for food during hard times would be a drain on the wolves' mental and physical resources. When following an injured target or a herd of animals the ability to travel some twenty miles or more in a day is only part of the story. The added resilience in attacking and overcoming a powerful prey that is about to lose his life, shows the capacity and tenacity of the wolf to achieve its objective.

This scenting ability is possibly one of the most important characteristics that ensured the survival of the wolf. Without an excellent sense of smell, distant prey on the correct side of the wind may not be detected. The invisible scent tracks of body odour from the hunted, plus the scent from crushed vegetation by the animal's movements would be a positive indication of a meal ticket at hand. To locate the ground scent of a passing animal would be important; but to determine the direction this animal had come from and was going would be vital to survival. For a wolf to follow the scent path in the wrong direction would end in frustration and greater hunger.

The environment of the time created the characteristics of the wolf and, therefore, the characteristics that were passed on to the domesticated species that preceded the dog. The introduction of man to their territories would effect changes to the environment. The wolves would learn to accept these changes.

Man, to feed his own family, would probably hunt the wolf. An enterprising wolf would consider children, with little means of defending themselves as easy prey. Man and wolf would be living in conflict, yet man did learn to make use of wolf pups and secure a social bond with suitable animals as they reached maturity.

Domestication of other suitable wild animals was also taking place and wolves began to feature for their contribution to hunting, guarding and herding. The taming and training of young wolves, along with selective breeding, would prove to be a significant advancement in the quality of early human life.

Domestication of other species of animals was for the prime purpose of supplying food and other materials that would improve the humans' standard of living. They were used to help with the hunting for meat and maintaining animals in captivity – the forerunners to our present farm livestock. The development of the domesticated dog played an important role in this process of evolution. This development from wolves by selective breeding into the early-domesticated dogs was well-established centuries before Roman times with the creation of three founder breed types – the hunting dog, the herding or shepherding dog and the guard dog.

It would appear that very early social groups within the human race kept, and brought up, very young wild animals. These youngsters would probably have lost their mothers and would have died if not taken in to an active community. Some would be playthings for the children and be looked after by the women. If these animals stayed within the community in adult life and bred under these circumstances, future generations became dependent on man, these animals would then be considered as domesticated.

The selectively bred wolves into the various species of early dog would be of assistance to the herdsman to manoeuvre or guard the newly domesticated livestock. With their ability to help the hunter, it will be seen how hunting, herding and guarding groups started to develop so that the various breeds became specialists at what they could do best to serve the needs of the primitive human communities.

The continuation of selection would result in the combinations of require-ments which would fertilise further specialisation. This can be said of many herding dogs where guarding also became an important feature. Guarding would involve the protection of a herd or flock against animal and human predators and also for the warning or defence of domestic abode or com-munity compounds. As for the hunting dogs, they would split up into breeds suitable for the various functions, such as flushing, pointing and retrieving.

It is often easier to visualise the requirements of today's domestic dogs by looking at the character of their origins – the wolf.

Chapter 3

UNDERSTANDING SITUATIONS

Dogs and their human companions

I consider that the most important characteristics within dogs and their owners would be – *dominance – submission – affection – fear*. When we look at the dogs themselves, each of these characteristics is inherited, to some degree or another, from wolf pack situations as we have seen. However, the human factor has to be added to complete the scenario.

Breeding for particular purposes will have created breeds of dogs with differing degrees of each of these characteristics, in fact, within any particular breed or even a litter there will be a difference in the amount of each characteristic that will make each dog unique. If we consider the variations in the environment from birth and the situation relating to each dog, to the owner and his family, the variations become more difficult to grasp.

Each of the four characteristics can also vary according to the situations in which a dog finds himself; past experiences will also affect a dog's response to a developing situation. A dog will have an amazing ability to assess his success or failure of the past, how it will affect the present and possibly the future.

A dog that has found that by taking a dominant stance, he has achieved a favourable result, will be encouraged to take a similar attitude in the future. However, if canine dominance has been countered, resulting in his own submission, he will think twice about trying it on again.

The foundation for training any dog is based on his action or reaction being happily accepted by his owner (or the party being involved with the dog at the time). The happy acceptance can be termed as affection – praise, titbits, fondling or the playing with toys. This will always be the easiest and quickest way to achieve a constructive (training) response. There may, of course, be occasions when owner dominance requires to be shown to achieve a submissive result from the dog. However, that result should never take away from the affection that should be shown to the dog immediately following success.

Inconsistencies

Many owners consider that their dogs are inconsistent in their reaction to a situation. One example is coming back when called, when dogs sometimes respond immediately and on other occasions, they just ignore any attempt at control. Owners do get exasperated when these situations arise and their reactions often make the situation more difficult to resolve.

I like to work on the premise that dogs are among the most consistent of animals, much more consistent than most owners who have not been tutored correctly on the subject. It is the situation or the memory of previous situations that create the change in reaction from a dog. Even if it is the smallest variation, such as a change in the owner's tone of voice can have an affect. It is a matter of perception from the dog's point of view, it is how the dog perceives each situation; what is happening at that moment and what he expects to happen if he responds or if he does not.

When looking at the recall, distance between dog and owner can play a vital role and the strength of distractions is a feature which is often ignored. Most of these factors are of less importance as the dog becomes fully trained to ignore distractions. However, an owner's inconsistencies and irritated displeasure will certainly affect a dog's reactions and can have a drastic affect on the progress to a controlled situation.

Human versus canine logic

This is where canine logic comes into play. The appreciation of canine logic is the initial step to understand the true nature of a dog's reactions. This can best be described as: 'A dog will always do what he considers to be in his best interest at that particular moment in time'.

It is important that we, as dog owners, think about our own actions and reactions as well as considering a dog's approach to life. It is rather unfortunate that human actions are often unconsciously geared to that of raising a family. The actions of dogs and children can be alike in so many ways especially young children at the toddler stage who are not yet able to express themselves verbally.

We all like to play with children; they like to be chased, with Mum or Dad pretending to run at great speed until finally catching up with the little one. As the toddler grows and runs away at the wrong moment, down a busy street or in a shopping precinct he can still be caught and gradually taught that there are times for fun and games and times to behave. When the language barrier has been broken and a toddler begins to speak, the youngster then begins to understand why he must not run away, he also understands the warnings or threats if he continues to misbehave.

Let us look at the same situation with a puppy. Puppies love games as much as children, puppies will chase each other just as grown dogs will continue with the fun of the chase in their adult life. If puppy owners take the place of litter mates and chase their young puppies in fun, where does it stop? Very young puppies are easily caught but in a matter of weeks they can outstrip their human elders or hide in corners that are quite inaccessible. When the puppy begins to feel a measure of independence and will not come when called, then serious chasing will begin, with the puppy enjoying the game, but the owner becoming frustrated and bad tempered because of his puppy's disobedience.

As this puppy grows up and continues, with greater skill to avoid capture, the final outcome is punishment at the hands of his owner. This usually results in a fit of human temper. Is it a wonder dogs do not understand human logic? This is only one example of a situation when people apply human thinking to the activities of a dog when it is based on the experience of children.

I think it is true to say that a young child who has not yet learnt to speak is probably on a similar mental plane as our dogs. Once a child has learnt to speak, the form of communication alters, and the understanding between child and adult reaches a level that could never be attained between dog and owner. The communication between a dog and his owner, because of the language barrier, always remains at a lower level. Although with practice and experience, it can reach a very sophisticated stage of perfection at that level.

A child who can communicate can understand praise and punishment. He can be warned of the consequence of any proposed failure to behave or obey. He understands delayed punishment, being sent to bed early when Dad has discovered some misdemeanour that occurred earlier in the day. This, a dog does not understand.

To try and explain to a dog that he is going to be punished if he does wrong, or to punish him after the event is not only a waste of time but helps to destroy the confidence he has in his owner. He cannot understand what is happening and will only become confused. A dog's level of understanding is based on what is pleasant and what is unpleasant; also on what he thinks caused the pleasant or unpleasant situation. Praise and punishment are not in his vocabulary.

A dog gets an ear nipped in the tailgate of the car as it is being closed, the pain and unpleasantness of the situation sticks in his memory and he will keep clear of it in future. Without this happening, a dog cannot be warned that he is likely to get his ear nipped and you cannot expect him to under-stand the reason for your warning. If he is spoken to in a manner that keeps him well away from the tailgate he will stay there because he has been commanded in an unpleasant manner. Without it actually happening, the possible tailgate injury does not affect his reasoning.

A wasp sting will bring out a variety of reactions the next time a dog hears another wasp. Some dogs will show respect and keep clear, others will show fear and hide, while still others will show aggression and will probably get stung again for their efforts. They may even be caught time and time again, but will feel the satisfaction of having disposed of a buzzing pain carrier.

What is sure, is that the dog will react each time he realises a wasp is close enough to cause unpleasantness. *Canine logic, is to react to his interpretation of the experience.*

To understand, and to continually think about canine logic, is the best way to appreciate why a dog reacts as he does at any time; especially when there is to be some form of communication from owner to dog.

Although human beings can be apportioned the same logic there are significant constrictions that will affect the dog owners' actions or reactions. The fact that human beings think on a different plain from a dog means that the human usually has a greater sense of responsibility. These are responsibilities of conscience, consideration and love of his dog, along with laws and regulations within the community that will always influence an owner's approach to situations that affect his dog.

Although canine loyalty and affection will influence a dog's response, his logic will be based on his instincts of survival.

Each dog has his strong and weak points within his character and these will affect his ability to be trained for certain specific purposes. However, these strengths and weaknesses will probably have been deliberately selected through a lengthy breeding programme. This can be experienced through the examination of dogs selected for work against dogs from the same breed being brought into the world specifically for breed showing. It is well known that the type of Labrador bred for the show ring, and most of the progeny who end up as domestic pets, is so different from the lean, muscular and highly alert Labrador that is bred for work with the gun. There are other breeds where the working potential is not recognised as important by most breeders and, within each generation, there is a degeneration of some of the genes required for a good and natural response to work.

With these dogs, it can be more difficult to achieve the standard of excellence expected from that breed. Much of my life has been taken up with the field of competition in Working trials where nose and protection work are important features. Tracking and searching are essential exercises, especially when combined with protection work for police dogs.

All dogs have the ability to track, but only some have the potential to master the art for high-grade professional or competitive work. Although some of those dogs without a real inclination for work can progress quite well when that little door in their brain box has been opened by a touch of training ingenuity.

Chapter 4

UNDERSTANDING OWNERS

Owners, like their dogs, also vary considerably in their abilities and with some there can be great difficulty in getting them to understand the importance of their own actions and involvement.

The character, temperament and understanding of the dog owner will have a great deal of influence on his dog's behaviour. His knowledge on the subjects of training and canine psychology are additional factors that help to complete the essential ingredients of successful owners.

Successful owners can be compared with parents who bring up well-behaved and considerate children. To achieve such ends, parents require to have their children's interests at heart, must be prepared to spend time in helping guide them into the future and should set a good example by their own attitude and consideration. They should also be prepared to act firmly and fairly to counter any deviation from the accepted path. With this in mind, the understanding between children and their parents may be different from the understanding required between a dog and his owner, but the basic principles are very similar.

As dogs vary considerably in character, temperament and inherited instincts it will be recognised that their owners a1so vary in a similar manner; although convention may be a controlling factor on the approach by many dog owners,

Some people can be very short of temper and impatient with a lack of consideration for their canine companions, and therefore cause a fair measure of distrust. Situations can develop where a dog will not be able to interpret his owner's requirements, nor will he be able to understand his changing moods.

Some owners can be rather indecisive or too tolerant and will generally find that their dogs take advantage of them. This can result in a fair measure of canine disobedience with dogs taking the initiative of pack leader. Other owners will take a dominating, an overbearing, or a ruthless approach to ensure that their dogs give an immediate response to their requirements, only to find that canine companionship has lost its pleasure for both parties. Yet others will treat their dogs as human beings giving them the credit of a full understanding of the human mind, as well as the human language. They then wonder why their dogs obey certain instructions but fail to act on others.

Each dog owner must learn to understand he will probably have his own failings. He should try to create a reasonable balance of patience and decisiveness, of understanding and consideration, also learning the strengths and weaknesses within his own dog.

I am making no claims to an educated background on psychology and my writings are based on experiences with dog owners, instructors and, to that of a normal working life. I think a lot can be learnt about people when helping to train their dogs and watching them within the domestic and competitive or operational environments. Human intelligence is not a critical feature; it is the ability, through natural and learned skills, that is more likely to highlight the variation in human capabilities.

Any introductory training procedure should be suited for the educational requirements of a puppy where a positive but gentle attitude will normally bring about the desired results. Situations could be adapted for the more adolescent or adult dog with a contrary attitude towards life. Training procedures should give prominence to basic requirements and, when achieved, this will create a foundation for a controlled companionship. It will also be the prime constituent for further development into one of the competitive or professional fields of work.

Some important principles

LOOKING AT YOURSELF

One never seems to think of skills and abilities when it comes to dog owner-ship, but in a sense, it is no different from gardening or carrying out domestic chores. Some people are naturally good at it and some are not, There is no sense in having a garden if you are not prepared to learn simple skills, apply your abilities, or increase your knowledge to get some benefit or pleasure from the garden rather than looking out on an eyesore. The same with house-hold chores: cleaning, cooking, redecorating and the like all take skills, ability and knowledge to maintain the home comforts we all like.

Dog ownership is no different, although the effects of the attributes already mentioned are of a broader concern within the community. Dog ownership involves a variety of activities and each contributes to the pleasures or displeasures of canine companionship. A broad classification of these activities could be:

1. Accommodation
2. Feeding
3. Exercising
4. Hygiene and Healthcare
5. Grooming
6. Training

7.   Handling and Control
8.   Recreation

Each of these activities can and will affect the general or specific behaviour of a dog, and therefore the degree of satisfaction by both owner and dog within this relationship. To achieve the desired level of companionship that an owner requires is dependant on the owner's ability to mould and control their canine companion's actions and reactions.

Many of the skills and abilities can be recognised as natural talents, some have been gained through day to day experiences while others are achieved through trial and error, Yet so many others are acquired with the assistance of other experienced parties.

What are these skills and abilities?

KNOWLEDGE

This subject probably covers the widest field with an endless list of categories; although they can probably be put into three broad subjects.

1.   The characteristics of the breed and of the dog itself.
2.   The basic to advanced training exercises and the techniques that are available.
3.   An early identification and recognition of problems.

The characteristics of the breed and of the dog itself

Owners should know as much as they can about their breed or the dogs that make up a crossbreed. Although much can be learnt from books on a breed, these books do not always tell of the weakness within the breed or within a particular line of breeding.

I recall many years ago when there was a problem with one of the country's most popular breeds. The Golden Retriever is one of the nicest dogs you could own, but it became apparent some years ago that a few had become overprotective of their own property and would even attack the people who loved them most – the owners. Be it food, a bone or a toy, possessiveness brought out a protective attitude and many owners did not anticipate or know how to handle the situations in its earliest stages. A small problem to start with became a nightmare to a number of owners. It appears that this trait came through one particular line that was doing well in the show ring. Happily, the problem now seems to have disappeared.

Many years ago Dr Roger Mugford highlighted, what he called the 'Rage Syndrome' in Cocker Spaniels. For a number of years the breeders denied the existence of such a condition. Without the knowledge of such situations, prospective owners could make a choice within this breed and be landed with quite a problem. Again, this condition now seems to have disappeared, but it caused a great deal of concern at the time.

There are a number of basic characteristics that can give a prospective owner food for thought, such as:

1. Knowing what Terriers were bred for is one example.
2. That Springer Spaniels are used to flush out game.
3. The various Sight Hounds were bred to accentuate the power of their eyesight. These hounds can distinguish movement at great distances and the use of this talent can encourage free-range movement. With Sight Hounds, some owners find the purpose of their dogs' breeding initially, to be a handicap; especially if they have not been taught at an early stage to come back when called.

Trainability of the dog for a chosen purpose in an owner's mind can make life much easier for any owner.

The basic training exercises

The basic training exercises along with the techniques available are factors that help pet dog owners to decide what training their dogs require for domestic control. Although training for more advanced, competitive or professional work will require more precise and thoughtful training, this will bring about its own rewards for these owners.

The knowledge and application of training techniques generally requires the knowledge from more than one source. The ability to assess the value of your sources of knowledge can be of great value. Few sources have the knowledge required for advising on a broad spectrum of activities and some are specialists in one field or type of technique only.

Early identification and recognition of problems

This is a very important aspect of any training programme. Unfortunately training seldom reaches its full objectives without some sort of problem coming to the fore; it is early identification that can help with a sound approach to solving, countering and learning from any mistakes or misjudgements that have been made.

DEXTERITY

An owner's physical mobility can help keep a dog alert to what is going on and, along with mental mobility, the owner can act or react to situations on demand. The owner's activity is meaningful to his dog if it is made with a purpose in mind, and if the dog understands that purpose. Each activity should have a meaning, probably short and sharp so that the dog's attention is more than just observant.

These activities could also come under the heading of communication and should be well co-ordinated between movement and sound, either vocal or the result of some other noise such as:

a clap of the hand
a stamp of the foot
the blowing of a whistle
the banging of metal tins
the use of a clicker
the rattle of a bunch of keys

There are of course others, but the above will give some idea of the manner in which a dog's attention can be attained or a specific canine action should take place.

Vocal noises can also be very numerous; they can be individual words with a specific meaning, phrases with or without a key word to indicate what is required from the dog. A single word is likely to be a positive instruction, and an unintelligible vocal expression may be a means of generating a dog's attention or creating a stop on some unwanted canine activity.

Dogs are likely to respond or not, to the manner in which physical or noise-orientated activities are presented to them. Any such physical or noise-orientated human activity will be taken as 'pleasant' or 'unpleasant' by the dog and it must be very clear in the owner's mind what he intends to convey to his canine friend.

Communicative

Although dexterity is an integral part of the system of communication the art of getting instructions through to dogs goes much further. There is no doubt that a dog who understands his owner's requirements is much happier, contented, and obedient than one which is confused, because of undefined or inconsistent signals which seem to be transmitted from his owner. It should also be recognised that there is a language barrier between man and dog and, unless the dog understands the meaning of a verbal instruction, he is not expected to respond as the owner intended.

The manner of an instruction may be by voice, an unusual sound, or by a physical movement. Inducements or physical assistance may initially be used to achieve the desired response from a dog before bringing in the final method of instruction. As an example, when training a dog to sit, it is quite useless to make use of the word 'sit' if he has not been properly introduced to the activity. *Dogs learn from actions not words.* To entice or physically induce your dog into the sit position will soon be understood as a meaningful activity being directed from the owner's actions. It is only when those actions are meaningful to the dog that he will learn to translate correctly the final means of communication by word or signal. If the owner wishes to use the word 'sit' as the final means of communication, this specific instruction only becomes of value after the dog knows how to carry out the activity as desired by the owner.

Another approach is to make use of the dog's natural desire to sit or go down.

A dog can eventually learn to sit or go down when instructed if he is requested to do so as he is carrying out the act of his own free will. However, I would not guarantee that the action would take place with a smart purpose in mind if that were the owner's requirement.

Sounds and actions from an owner are there to tell the dog something, but he will only react to the owner's wishes if he has correctly translated their meaning. To do so, these sounds and actions must be consistent to ensure a proper understanding. Inconsistency from an owner can only create a confused dog.

Anticipation

This is a two-way situation. The owner's anticipation of the dog's next action or activity and also the dog's anticipation of the owner's next action or activity. A dog is much better at anticipating his owner's activities, than an owner is at his dog's next move.

Without a dog's ability to anticipate, he could not be so easily trained. There are examples of anticipation every day, and if we were to study them, we should appreciate the connecting link between each phase in the build up to a dog's actions. He knows when he is going to be taken out last thing at night. The owner kicks off his slippers and the dog knows that he is going to put on his shoes. He gets off his chair and goes for his dog's lead. The dog will probably be there with tail wagging before the owner. Each of the owner's actions is anticipated because the owner has built up the regular programme of events that he has unconsciously developed.

Anticipation in competitive work is probably the biggest 'crime' a dog can commit. When it happens, it is because this tremendous advantage has not been appreciated and kept in control. Controlled anticipation should be used to build up the power behind a dog's desire to carry out the function the owner has set in motion.

The nature in which the owner communicates, his voice or his mannerisms will also tell the dog what is coming next. If he has enjoyed it in the past, he will be happy to anticipate what is coming in the future, but if the past has caused displeasure he may unwillingly co-operate because he sees no alternative, or he may just opt out.

Canine logic will always kick in.

Observant and perceptive

Owners should be conscious of any situation that is developing, or likely to develop in a manner that will affect a dog's activity or performance.

Many an unwanted situation can be avoided if an owner is sufficiently observant to anticipate a likely situation. Sometimes it is the dog's perception of a noise, a movement or the scent in the wind that has created an alertness that should not be missed. There are other occasions when the owner's observation has picked up a more distant distraction that may come his way and cause a problem. He should be aware of these possible distractions.

When out for a walk a dog may stop with ears alert, and will swing round to pick up and concentrate on a source. If this could mean trouble, the observant owner can prepare himself and take the preventive action he feels would be advisable. It is the same with the owner who may pick up a probable distraction while his dog is quite unaware of the possibilities. Again avoiding action can be prepared in case this perceived problem becomes a reality.

It is the same when training for domestic control, competition or a professional field of work. An observant owner can visualise, and probably know from past experience, that a dog is likely to act undesirably and make a mistake. As one mistake can easily lead to another, it is better that preventive measures are taken at the most appropriate time.

One good example is while training for 'on or off lead' walking – this can be for domestic, or more advanced work. During a training session and while the dog is walking at heel (at owner's left side), any deviation from the owner's route can firstly be noted by the movement of the dog's eyes. Because the dog is in line with or slightly ahead of the owner this is unlikely to be noted, but the next indication is that of the head moving in the direction of the distraction; the body is likely to follow the head unless the training is of a standard to cope with the situation. If the distraction is straight ahead, a tightening of the neck or body muscles will give the indication of a distraction.

The most effective time to avoid canine inattention is when the eyes take in the cause. The next effective time is when the head moves. After that moment the opportunity to prevent body movement is probably lost. It should therefore be recognised that inattention is likely to start when the eyes deviate and be closely followed by head movement or body muscle tightening. This takes up a very short time span, probably one or two seconds at the most. Any failure of owner observation and immediate counteraction will be awarded with an unwanted intrusion into the dog's attention or performance.

Observation can only be partly effective if the owner does not have the perception to appreciate and act against the likely consequences.

Observation and perception can be equally effective when it is seen that the dog is going to do something that pleases the owner. The immediate recognition of this action can help with the training of many situations. As already mentioned the simplest situation is teaching a dog to sit when instructed. Each time a dog sits of his own accord a helpful word from the owner to sit is followed by praise. This will help with the training process.

There is much more to be written on this subject under another heading and related to the application of an individual dog's inherited instincts.

Adaptability

With such a wide variation from dog to dog and from owner to owner a precise and preconceived approach to training is not practical. Programmes and targets certainly have their place and are of great value, but the time scale for progress is more of an individual assessment.

Some dogs have an inherited aptitude to certain aspects of training and some dogs can have virtually none in others. Some are very early in maturing and will advance quickly, while with other aspects of training, a very slow and painstaking approach will be required to achieve progress.

Being prepared to make changes in an approach to training is important, not necessarily to change the programme but a small change in a technique can be as effective as aborting one approach for another. There are occasions when golden rules have to be broken (or temporarily suspended) to achieve realistic progress.

Long-term interests may have to be reconsidered to ensure that a block on progress has been overcome. Some dogs will flourish when training covers a narrow band of exercises where others would be bored. The same can be said for owners. It is generally found that it is the bored owners who finish up with bored dogs. Although a solid foundation in the exercises being trained is essential there are times when working for that foundation is the excuse to look for perfection in the shortest possible time.

The ability to apply adaptability comes with experience and it is often the adaptability of a fertile mind that comes to the rescue. Nothing (except cruelty) should be ruled out when considering changes to achieve success.

Confidence

An air of confidence combined with the ability to apply the various skills and abilities can only help to give a dog the confidence that he can achieve success with reliability.

Confidence without the signs of arrogance will always have a better chance of bringing out the right approach, but that confidence must never blind an owner to mistakes that might occur somewhere within a training programme. This is especially so when an owner is prepared to accept that any training hiccups or the performances are not the fault of the dog. An owner must always look closer to home for the causes of any deficiency.

Patience

Patience to build up and consolidate at each stage of training is important. Owners, when reaching a specific stage in training, often feel that the dog should immediately be taken on to the next stage. There are circumstances when this may have no adverse effect, but a period, albeit a short one, of consolidation will certainly benefit the stages of progression that are to follow.

This period of consolidation not only gives the dog the opportunity to become accustomed to his new learning but allows the owner to bring in variations, such as distractions, to help create versatility and the maintenance of canine attention.

When problems or the likelihood of them come to the surface, patience should again be applied to work out the root of the predicament rather than trying to use a 'quick fix' to achieve progress.

Patience with a dog that is slower than expected is a virtue, but should not be overdone if it is felt that the dog is taking advantage of situations. Although it is never a good policy for an owner to lose his temper with his dog I have, on occasions, found it necessary to ask an owner having a difficult time, to pretend he has run out of patience and apply this loss in a controlled manner. There is no such thing as a controlled situation when a person does run completely out of patience (loss of temper). He may regret his actions, but his dog's confidence will also have suffered badly.

Dogs are always capable of finding a weakness in the armoury of their owners, especially when patience is not suitably balanced.

Organise

The ability to plan a sequence of training situations or the application of techniques will be very beneficial. It is always easier to remember or see from the records what and how things have been done in the past. The planning and execution of intermediate training targets will certainly help to maintain an organised mind.

Motivation

An owner should always have a reason for wanting to train his dog. It may be to prevent problems or to cure them, to ensure that he brings up a well-behaved dog, or for the enjoyment of an educated partnership. Some owners may decide from the start that their goal is to progress into advanced work for a more professional or competitive basis. There are also occasions when basic control training can be combined with the introductory elements of advanced work.

Having an objective and seeing satisfactory results encourages motivation and leads to an enthusiastic outlook.

Sympathy

An ounce of sympathy from an owner under the right conditions can be a sign of considerate handling. However, sympathy at the wrong time can give the dog the impression that he can play on the softer feelings of his owner.

Humour

All activities in life benefit from a sense of humour and dog training is no different, so long as this sense of humour is never at the expense of the dog.

A happy and smiling face coming from his owner is all that many dogs need to put them in the right frame of mind.

It should be recognised that each of these particular skills and abilities are interrelated and a deficiency in one can negate the value of many others.

The partnership (To help complete this part of the picture.)

To enjoy a dog's company to the full he must be well behaved, have a bit of spirit – yes, to enjoy his life under his master's roof – yes, to be considered a member of the family – yes, but in his proper place. A dog is a pack animal by nature; he is either the pack leader or just a member of the pack finding his own place in the pecking order. Within the family, he can only be a member of the pack, and his place in the pecking order *must* be below the other members of the family. Brought up correctly, treated fairly, with consideration and encouraged to enjoy his life, he will understand his place in the community, just as nature intended.

Although the dog owner must be the pack leader, the relationship can be treated more as a partnership, with the dog as the junior and the human as the senior member of the partnership. It must be recognised that dogs know their owners better than owners know their dogs, or

Fun with the ball.

themselves. Dogs seem to be capable of analysing all our strengths and weaknesses; they have much more time than we have to carry out this analysis very successfully.

The true loyalty of a dog to his owner has got to be earned. The goodwill, which is built up between dog and owner, can be likened to a bank balance, with the dog's loyalty being measured in a similar manner to that of a bank manager to a client. A bank manager's loyalty is built on confidence and any overdraft is granted on his assessment of the client's ability to honour his debts. The expectation of loyalty from a dog is based on 'goodwill as the currency the dog understands'. To go too deep into debt with a dog, without him feeling that the situation will improve, will certainly damage any loyalty already built up and do great harm to the partnership.

It should be recognised that the dog is never at fault. He is a product of man's effect on breeding, on the dog's upbringing, also subsequent conditioning and training, The dog is the result of the owner's choice, the environment in which he has lived and on the owner's approach to his environment. The owner must accept full responsibility for any of his failings.

Chapter 5

UNDERSTANDING COMMUNICATION

The art of communicating is that the other party is able to understand your requirements before he can respond to you. If you are speaking to another human being by means of a common language, there should not be any problems. Unfortunately, even with such a simple example there are so many occasions when people pick up the wrong message, or the interpretation of the message is moulded to suit their own frame of mind.

If we start by giving thought to communication between two people who have no knowledge of each other's language, or that only one has the ability to hear, sign language becomes the principal means of communication. How often have we seen a foreigner with little appreciation of our language ask for directions to his destination? The use of hands, arms and any other physical movement is applied, if the question is not understood in the first place.

We also have a similar situation with a child who has not yet learnt to speak. Hands, arms, facial expressions and noises of various sorts play a large part in the process of communication along with the teaching process of words.

Even without the problem of a language barrier misunderstandings between two colleagues, friends or relatives are common place. How often is there a variety of interpretations from a discussion or even a simple instruction?

If it can be acknowledged that human beings are often far from perfect in communicating between one and another, it will be recognised that a great deal of thought must be given to the art of communicating with a dog.

Many people seem to believe that their dogs have an inherent knowledge of the language we speak and that they understand. How often do we hear owners repeating the word 'heel', and the dog does not play a blind bit of attention. How often do we hear a dog being given the command to 'sit'; and yet he does his own thing. So many owners do not realise that words in themselves are of no value, until the dog associates these words with particular actions. Even with today's knowledge, there are instructors who do not seem to appreciate the learning mechanism within a dog. It should also be recognised that *most of a dog's learning is not by design*, but by the environment in which he lives, by the rewards, or the unpleasant realities of day to day living. This, I shall call 'Incidental' learning. He learns that by jumping up on his owner and others the social contact gives its own rewards – good or bad. He learns to pull on the lead, because it gives him a sense of control; he has taken the Alpha status.

Dogs learn through repetition and consistency, where patience and consideration are very valued attributes in a dog owner. He has three principle senses that act as a connecting link between an owner's requirements, and his ability to receive and understand the messages.Those senses are hearing, seeing, feeling. The sense of smell is also very important to the dog and can certainly be used for communication and training, but that sense is not relevant at this stage.

The dog learns from our actions – with a pleasant experience they will respond to it. Unfortunately, under some trainers, he may have to learn that, if he does not react favourably, this will result in a very unpleasant experience. However, in a well-coordinated training routine we would only start to combine meaningful verbal instructions along with our actions when these actions have been well established. This will achieve the connecting link between the owner's action and the verbal instruction. A verbal instruction, at the earliest stages is likely to give a novice owner false expectancy of early success. This will result in some degree of frustration to many owners – their expectations are not being fulfilled.

As an example, the owner in the photograph is using a titbit close to the dog's nose to draw the head up in a manner that develops into the sit position. At the same time she would speak to him with a soothing voice and possibly in the form of a question.

Something like this, 'That's a good boy, are you going to sit for me?'.

Inducing a dog to sit with the use of titbits.

As he responds to her actions, the dog would immediately receive the titbit along with verbal praise, such as 'You are a clever boy'. Both titbits and praise would be his reward.

The word 'sit' would be lost within the initial sentence, but by the process of minor changes it would eventually become a verbal and single word of instruction to 'sit'. This would only happen when the initial routine had been established and with a consistent response. It is a gradual process from an informal approach to one of a positive single word instruction.

That would be my general approach, but there are occasions when a more positive and more demanding situation would be developed from the start. That is another story.

The dog should not be blamed for any failure to understand, but any such failure should result in a reappraisal of the approach to communication.

Sign language and physical assistance along with other inducements are very important aspects of dog training, especially in the earlier stages of each instruction being taught.

This understanding should be the starting point for any attempt by an owner to communicate with his dog. Dogs learn principally from actions; the meaning of words follow. However, the tone of voice, without understanding the meaning of the words, will certainly have an influence on a dog's reaction.

The expression of 'No, don't do that!' with a degree of verbal unpleasantness will stop a dog, a child, or a foreigner in their tracks, without an understanding of the expression itself. Their attention has been generated. The manner and timing in which the follow up is presented will then start to give the initial expression the attention it deserves. To do nothing more about it will give the impression that those sharp words were quite meaningless and it will not take long before such an approach is completely ignored. However, if the follow up is meaningful to the dog (and others) he will appreciate its value, and his memory of the situation will start to have the desirable affect on his future activities.

It is the repetition of the situation that eventually has the dog anticipating and responding. There are, of course, 'one off' situations that have immediate and lasting effects on a dog.

Unfortunately, so many of these are caused by unpleasant situations. If a dog catches his ear or tail in the tailgate of a car, that sharp and painful experience will probably last a lifetime and he will make sure that it will never happen again. The tailgate will get the blame. Not the person shutting it. If a dog gets a hiding from his owner for not returning when called he will not relate this unpleasant happening to staying away. However, he will relate it to his eventual return and to the creator of this unpleasantness. After that, it will not matter who calls him back in the future, there will be a degree of reluctance to go back to any party making the call. One person can cause apprehension in the dog's mind and others, who try at a later date, may wonder why the dog is so reluctant to respond to the simple instruction to come back when called.

Our every movement or utterance tells a dog something, but he will only pick out the activities that are of value to him. Unintentional communications are most obvious when his meals are being prepared or when the 'old man' puts on his shoes for the final walk of the evening. His dog may appear to be asleep, but activities of this nature will communicate his master's intentions and he will react accordingly.

To take this matter further we can illustrate by a good example of 'Incidental' learning'.This is from an owner's customary activities within daily routines that play a major role in his dog's build up of knowledge. Let us take the final routine of the 'old man' who puts on his shoes for the final walk of the evening.

1. He kicks off his slippers.
2. He puts his shoes on.
3. He get out of his comfy armchair.
4. He goes through to the hall and puts his coat on.
5. He goes to the kitchen and picks up the dog's lead.
6. He calls the dog and opens the back door.
7. The dog is now with his owner and ready to go out.

If this happens to yourself, think of how long it takes your dog to realise that when you are kicking off your slippers he is to be taken out. In a relatively short time he will have connected every element of your actions one by one; responding initially to element (4), then to (3) and then through to (2) and (1) .

If you happen to comment before putting your shoes on, 'It's time to take the old boy out', he will be there in a flash waiting. Dogs learn from actions, incidental or designed, then words have a meaning.

Dogs learn principally from repeated events, from pleasant and unpleasant situations. It is fully recognised that dogs are taught by repeating an activity and then being rewarded for a satisfactory response. Dogs also learn eventually, that a poor response from them, will result in no reward from the owner. How quickly they learn depends on the intelligence of the dog, the suitability of the training and the effect of that particular experience.

Dogs learn through self-interest and self-preservation. If their actions result in a pleasant experience, then under similar circumstances they are likely to respond out of self-interest (it does not take a dog long to realise when his meal is being prepared for him).

Dogs are often credited with the ability to read the thoughts of their owners, but their ability to anticipate is probably due to the fact that they can string together the activities of their owner where an unconscious word or action alerts the dog to the sequence which is likely to follow. The time of day also triggers off the expectation of certain activities which are of value to him. Every success in teaching a dog to do something when and where the owner requests it, is another break through the language barrier between teacher and pupil.

This brings us back to the previously mentioned canine logic – 'A dog will always do what he considers to be in his best interest at that particular moment in time'. The art of communicating is about asking and getting the desired response. You ask a dog to do something and he does it. You ask him to stop doing something and he stops.

There are many times when this asking is in the form of a non-compromising command, and in others, it may just be a click with your fingers, or some other minor movement or noises to have the dog happily carry out a simple request.

The manner in which an owner communicates with his dog makes the difference between complete failure and the degree of success. Everything that is done with a dog is dependent on the manner in which communication is applied.

Pleasantness and unpleasantness are the key instruments in the process of learning. A high degree of unpleasantness can be a very important feature in curing problems that are likely to be of danger to life or limb. A more time consuming and less unpleasant route can be taken with the same end result – if the dog lives long enough. When life and limb are at stake, the shortest possible route can become a necessity, but it should always be followed by a period of consolidation to be certain of a satisfactory result, and with a happy dog.

This chapter has only given the foundation for communicating and, although the next chapter describes the various aspects of control through communication, everything else in the book involves the transmission of the owner's wishes to his dog in the manner that he will understand.

Communicating is one thing, but the owner's recognition of a successful or unsuccessful transmission is equally important. A successful response from the dog is generally recognised with ease. However, the reasons for failure may not be so easy to understand. There is a chapter at a later stage, which should help with the assessment of failure or limited success.

Chapter 6

ASPECTS OF COMMUNICATION

At times, a dog's life must be rather difficult. A well-known saying by wayward husbands is 'my wife does not understand me'. If a dog could speak, we may hear him say 'my owner does not understand me'.

However, if we can accept and fully understand canine logic which was previously given as 'A dog will always do what he considers to be in his best interest at that particular moment in time', we will appreciate a dog's point of view. This means that a dog cannot be blamed or judged to be at fault for any action that is considered by human beings to be undesirable. No doubt an explanation will be expected for such a statement.

This statement may or may not be one hundred per cent accurate, but if we accept it as a fact of life, we are much more likely to find the cause for any canine activity. If we cannot blame the dog or consider him to be at fault, we must look for alternatives to that of canine punishment. We must also consider that to blame the dog would be to divert the responsibility from the proper source.

If we do not blame the dog, where does the responsibility rest? It may be in his breeding. It may be in his early upbringing. It may be due to his present environment.

Each of these factors brings us back to human beings. Man was responsible for the dog's breeding, even if it was accidental. Man was responsible for the pup's upbringing and what happened during his early life in the nest. Man chose his canine companion for life in his past living conditions, his new home and present environment. Each of these activities, created by man, has helped to create the dog's present behaviour. At the end of the day, the dog owner must accept responsibility for his present charge and may unwittingly or indirectly be responsible for being landed with his present activities, good or bad.

If the dog cannot be blamed for his so called misdemeanours, he is not an offender and, as I have already said, should not be punished. It may be difficult to accept that dogs do not understand punishment, but he will recognise an *unpleasant* situation and, with the correct timing, he can relate this *unpleasantness* with the activity he is carrying out. To some people, this may be just another expression for punishment, but a failure to fully understand the difference between punishment and *unpleasantness* will only lead to an inappropriate human frame of mind with its improper use or timing.

To quote Colonel Konrad Most in his book, *Training Dogs – A Manual* 'a dog cannot, in the true sense of the word, be praised or blamed, rewarded or punished. We can only do something that is agreeable or disagreeable to him'.

If a dog is doing something that displeases you, this can be countered by doing something that is *unpleasant* (disagreeable) to him. If, on the other hand, his activity is to your liking and, especially if you want to make use of it in the future, then an immediate *pleasurable* (agreeable) act from yourself will be remembered and should meet with his approval.

We should not use the expression of –

(1) Blame (against the dog)
(2) Punishment (of the dog)

Nevertheless, we should understand (3) Praise or (4) Reward as an appreciation of approved canine activities.

The first two expressions can give the wrong impression of the situation. If there is a source for blame the owner should look, not at the dog, but else-where, probably at himself, his environment, or training routines.

The use of the word punishment, whether intended or not will always be directed against the dog because he is considered to have done something wrong and the owner's reaction is likely to be applied incorrectly. If and when there is a situation that requires a 'disagreeable' act against the dog, this *unpleasantness* must be applied with the frame of mind and the timing of the action to suit that particular occasion.

The third and fourth expressions 'praise and reward' are not recognised as such by the dog. However, they are recognised by us, and the dog, as a very *pleasant* experience.

I may be using double standards by recommending the continued use of the words 'praise' and 'reward' instead of discarding them for the alternative – *pleasant*. Although praise is actually one form of reward, these expressions can only do well when applied correctly and will be used along with *pleasant* throughout this book.

A *pleasant* owner reaction at just the right time will help to induce the desired canine response and an *unpleasant* owner reaction at just the right time will help to terminate an unwanted canine activity.

The timing is from best to least effective time for a human response and that can be taken from the time the dog is thinking of acting in a certain manner to the time he has completed his action. To take action two seconds after completion is too late and is unlikely to have any affect.

If a dog is picking up his ball and you give *pleasant* encouragement to do so, he will recognise your enthusiasm and should respond accordingly.

However, if your dog is picking up one of your shoes and you verbally hit him with a short and sharp reproach, he will recognise the *unpleasantness* of the situation and will be stopped in his tracks. In each case, what you do next and when you do it will determine the lesson he has gained from the situations.

Unpleasantness

Generally speaking, unpleasant reactions to your dog should be short and sharp with the degree of unpleasantness that is going to put a stop on his undesirable activity. When the dog has stopped, he is acting in a manner that suits you. That reaction deserves praise (pleasantness) as recognition for his co-operation. However, it should not stop at that; getting a reward for doing nothing has, in itself, little meaning to him. If you were to walk away and leave him, there is a fair chance that he would go back to the undesirable activity. A follow up is necessary and that can be anything that suits the owner and dog and the situation.

Your dog is chewing the corner of the rug and you catch him. An uncompromising hit with your voice may only be your dog's name or 'what are you doing?' so long as it gets his attention. He stops and looks at you, your response should be immediate with 'that's a good boy' in a pleasing soft tone and followed with something really pleasant, such as, 'come on son, where is your box of toys?' or 'come on son, I have a biscuit for you'. You can have a short session of fun or some more titbits (or both) to take his attention away from the rug in the nicest way.

Unpleasantness is short and sharp; pleasantness is drawn out with excitement or a soothing atmosphere. A repeat of the whole procedure as and when necessary will do a lot to cure the problem. However, any attempt by the dog to chew the rug in the future must be stopped immediately as he is going to it. If he is allowed the pleasure of chewing that item again, this will ruin all your previous work and it will become more difficult to achieve a long-term positive result. Such a problem may require a bit more thought, such as removing the rug completely for a period of time or to spray a deterrent on the offending corner.

Pleasantness

When an owner wishes to encourage his dog to continue doing something that pleases him, this is another matter.

As an example, when your dog is coming to you of his own free will, it is an ideal opportunity to assist your training programme. On occasions like this give your dog all the encouragement you can along with the instruction you will give in times of need. 'Come on son, that is a good boy' or something similar, with a suitably pleasant tone of voice, is all that is required to show your pleasure at his action. The immediate follow up can be a reward of fun and games, a titbit, or both. What is important is that he is sharing with your pleasure.

Understanding requirements

A dog must be able to understand his owner's requirements and activities before he can be expected to respond correctly. These desires are projected in various ways, but can be grouped within the following

Physical restraint
By feel
By sound
By visual means
With training aids
Any combination of above

The dog must correctly translate these activities to achieve the desired response.

OWNER ACTIVITIES

Physical restraint
This can be by means of equipment such as a collar and lead or by manhandling in a manner that prevents the dog from carrying out a function of his own design.

By feel

The minimum application of equipment attached to a dog, such as a collar and lead for a means of communication when it is required. Also light body or hand contact in a manner which, on its own or augmenting other means of communication, to achieve the desired canine activity.

By sound

This generally indicates vocal instructions (words) but can also include any meaningful noise such as

(i)   Clap of the hands or stamp of the feet
(ii) Use of a whistle
(iii) Unintelligible noises from the vocal cords

By visual means
Normally this will encompass a full range of physical activities which can be seen by the dog and involve

(i)   Hands and fingers
(ii) Arms
(iii) Body movements
(iv) Head movements and eye contact

Drawing attention by visual means.

With training aids

Training aids are usually applied to control a dog's behaviour or to introduce a particular training activity. Many of these aids can be utilised for both training activities and behaviour control, they can be listed as

- (i) Equipment such as collars and leads of various kinds and any specialised items such as trailing lines and activity cords
- (ii) Play toys
- (iii) Titbits of food

Any combination of above

Although any combination can and should be considered to achieve the desired action or reaction from a dog, there should not be any dependence on one single type of activity at any time. It should also be appreciated that a dog will generally learn from the owner's physical actions. The relevance of specific words or sounds becomes meaningful after the specific activity is understood by the dog. There are, however, exceptions where specific noises or words can be utilised as a foundation for generating a dog's attention. One example is the use of the dog's name.

It is how and when owner activities are applied, with variations in vocal control along with physical activities, which induce the desired responses from our dogs. A controlled companionship should be the foundation of a happy one.

Focussing attention

Communicating is about creating and achieving a focus for the dog's immediate attention on the communicator himself. Having achieved that focus of attention, some act of interest to the dog must immediately be carried out to give purpose for drawing the dog's attention in the first place. It is the satisfaction of both dog and owner that is the pivotal point in this important act of communicating.

Initially, the point of focus is likely to be the owner's face – his eyes or/and mouth; source of the vocal cords. The owner's hands may also be a focal point for the dog – if the hands have been used intelligently as an area of attention generation. This can be described as 'elementary focusing' and the attention generating process can change in accordance with the experience of the dog to his owner. If a dog can detect any specific follow up action, the elementary focusing on the owner may barely exist before the dog takes up the position in readiness for the next instruction.

These focal points of attention may eventually vary according to the situation and the owner's follow up activity. Initially, the focal point will be on the owner's person, but experience creates anticipation and the dog can leave out this focal point. Although more will be written about anticipation at a later stage, this is a very important factor in dog ownership, behaviour analysis and training.

Dogs with 'best' friends or relatives of their owners who do not live in, brings out an example. An owner can see one of these canine 'best' friends coming up the road to pay a visit and he just says to the dog, who may even be in another room, 'Here's your Uncle Bob coming to see you', with emphasis on the Uncle Bob. The dog will be there in a flash at the door or the window to see and welcome his 'best' friend.

In training and during competitions I have found it beneficial to say, 'Come on son, are we going for a *track*' or some other suitable exercise. He knows the joy of the exercise, is raring to go, and is looking for indications of where we are going.

I recall one Working trials competitor who was being called to carry out the Search exercise. He was a fellow who had his dog right under his thumb, and was a bit of a show off. Normally, when taken out of the car, the dogs are put on the lead then walked to the search area. The dogs usually know what is going on, love the exercise and pull the owners to the working area.

On this occasion, the owner got his dog out of the car, did not put the lead on the dog, but he did let us see an excellent piece of heel off lead in his one hundred yard walk to the search area. When the dog was commanded into the working area he appeared to be dead from the neck up and kept looking at his owner with as much as to say, 'Ho NO, not again!'

Although it is important to have a dog fully controlled by his owner when it is required, the procedure can be taken too a degree that affects his ability to see beyond that immediate requirement.

Vocal communication

Most communicating is carried out by our vocal cords. The variation in the use of the voice and their effect requires explaining.

Most people find it easy to use voice fluctuation when looking after the interests of children. Soft encouraging tones do much to gain their interest and let them know they are doing well. That encouraging tone can also be changed in a split second into a short, sharp 'No' as a stopper for a child whose actions are creating imminent danger to himself. A child goes too near to a fire or is in the act of taking pills (medicine) that look like sweets. The shock of the 'No' stopper is then immediately followed by endearments for taking notice of the urgent attention generator.

It is the same with dogs, where the variations are used and altered in a split second from one extreme to another as the situations demand. With both dogs and children, it is important to finish with endearments to illustrate genuine fondness and appreciation for their cooperation.

When working with dogs, voice fluctuation can be very similar to application with children. Unfortunately, when wrongly applied it results in creating a number of spoilt children in this world; spoilt dogs come from the same type of source.

COMMANDS – INSTRUCTIONS – REQUESTS

Unfortunately, the use of the expression 'command' is far too common. In the field of competition within Obedience and Working trials the Kennel Club makes the word 'command' the prominent means of instructing a dog throughout their regulations. This is principally by the use of an 'extra command' and when it can or cannot be used, in other situations there is the use of the expression 'last command'.

Because of the official prominence of these expressions, instructors at training clubs and some writers of articles or books on related subjects use the expression as if there was no other way of putting the message through to the owner and, consequently the dog. To use the word so freely there is a danger of applying a demanding approach when it is not appropriate. I do recognise that some instructors use the word 'command' as a figure of speech without applying it in a draconian manner.

Dogs do not like to be 'commanded' any more than we do. Human life, either domestic or commercial, would be no life at all if all instructions or requests were issued in the form of commands. There are times when we have to obey a command, but this is usually when there has been a lack of application by one side or another, or the need to act in a more responsible manner.

I suppose it applies to humans as well, but I believe when dealing with dogs commands should normally be applied as a 'stopper' to prevent or stop a dog from carrying out a function that does not suit us. A command is a form of compulsion.

To understand why instructions and requests are of greater value than commands requires an understanding of the basic objectives. We wish to control our dogs or train them for specific objectives, and do so with dogs that are enjoying life to the full. We wish to finish with dogs that are very keen to please, dogs that know we appreciate everything they do for us. The principal consideration is to use an approach that finally creates dogs with a real desire to please.

I would like to explain that the response we expect from a trained dog is a reflection on our own attitude to dogs and their training. If we are demanding and lacking in consideration, we are likely to have dogs that do as they are told, but will probably be devoid of much of their natural character. If owners are firm but fair, full of encouragement, construct their training in a manner so that the dogs enjoy these sessions, owners should finish with eager dogs, which are full of character.

We want to train in a manner where the dogs are being released to carry out our requests. We want the dogs to carry out a trained exercise and the routine where they do not require to be told to carry it out, but to release by the owner so that the dog's knowledge and great desire takes them into and through the procedure.

When an owner want his dog's undivided attention or have him remain in a stationary (static) position, he is instructed. There should, however, be sufficient edge in the owner's voice to achieve the desired effect. When the owner wishes to develop and create an active canine situation, he is requested to do so. It is in fact a release to do what is asked of the dog and he is willing to do it.

Remember, a command can be considered as an act of compulsion – 'the dog does it or else'.

While giving instructions or making requests, the dog usually learns from the owner's actions and then learns to carry them out from the vocal application. It will be seen that the instruction or request is often carried out from the owner's visual indication without the need to use the vocal application.

There are times in the early stages of training, conditioning, or during sessions of retraining, when a more demanding approach is required. Although this will be dealt with at a later stage, everything that is done is based on finishing with dogs that are full of character and are happy to oblige with the owner's requirements.

Vocal communication is probably central to the art of dog training, but the voice can also be helpful when used in conjunction with the other means available. Other forms of noise control can also be utilised, the clap of the hands, the stamp of the feet can be very effective in gaining the dog's attention. A whistle can be very useful, especially when distance and wind can take the effectiveness out of your voice. Gundog people and shepherds make excellent use of the whistle and its variations to communicate their instructions to their dogs.

The household pet can be easily trained to identify a small number of instructions via the whistle. Two examples are, to have the dog to come when called or to stay where he is. It must be remembered that the use of the whistle is used when he already understands the function expected from him.

Visual signals can also supplement, or be used to great effect along with, vocal means of communication. There are so many combinations that can be applied when communicating with a dog and these animals can respond to more than one form of instruction. Fuller details of their use will be brought in later in these writings.

Chapter 7

UNDERSTANDING INDUCEMENTS

There are many inducements (or incentives) in the field of dog training and there are many ways of applying these inducements.

Although it is not generally recognised as such, compulsion is an inducement and a logical application in a number of circumstances. These days many instructors and behaviourists consider that compulsion and inducements are miles apart and do not come into the same category.

However, if we fully understand and recognise compulsion as a form of inducement, good, sound and acceptable applications will be applied. The draconian and unpleasant side of compulsion involving mental or physical torment is not an option that is considered within these writings.

Instead of using the expression 'compulsion' for the good and sound practices that can be demanding, I would prefer to use the expression of being 'authoritative' when making an urgent requirement on a dog's cooperation.

The expression of inducements will now be used for any training approach that requires a more stimulating outlook from owner to dog. On many occasions both authoritative and inducement orientated approaches cannot be kept apart and must be used in conjunction with each other to achieve the cooperation that results in success.

If we consider that to command is to apply compulsion, be it by vocal or physical application, it is to apply an authoritative approach.

To gain a dog's attention, especially when there is a distraction that is taking his interest, an authoritative tone of voice will probably be required. However, to maintain that attention and do something with it, a more accommodating inducement will be used to complete a successful situation.

Let me explain this. In the early stages of training we can look into the Sit and Down positions. These may well be achieved by using the kindest of inducements, but to keep him there will require an authoritative outlook mixed with praise for complying, while ensuring that the dog does not change position because of that praise.

There are many situations within the fields of domestic, competitive or professional training where these combinations are successfully applied. This will be demonstrated more fully at a later stage during the approach to training the basic control exercises.

Titbits, toys and gadgets

Titbits, toys and gadgets as training aids are only of real value if they are helping to ensure an owner is in control of his dog. However, it is often forgotten that they are just 'training aids'. They are there to help create a situation where the owner can take control in their absence. There are of course exceptions, and these can be of value when a dog or owner finds it advisable to supplement his approach to training.

The use of titbits is, because they can be a good inducement, most likely to minimise the personal commitment of the owner and it is a very serious concern of mine. Having watched so many owners making use of titbits, it is obvious that a high proportion think that is the limit of their involvement during constructive training or the elimination of behaviour problems. The titbit achieves an immediate result, but unfortunately, when the titbit is not forth-coming these owners seem to be quite unable to appreciate why the dog does not respond as they had in the past. Owners must be taught how, when and why, along with the back up of personal inducements and encourage-ment to achieve cooperation from the dog.

I recall one client in a training class when I was introducing the owners to the use of titbits and this gentleman refused to use them. His reason was that he wanted the dog to 'work' for him, not for pieces of food. His ideal was perfectly sound and, as an instructor (and owner myself), I had to agree with his principals. Unfortunately, he did not have the ability at this early stage in training to apply inducements from the heart and tended to be demanding and dictatorial with his dog. At this stage, it was my objective to create a happy dog, one that wanted to show pleasure in what he was doing and to achieve the same with the owner. At the end of the day I failed, I could not get this owner to appreciate that his own attitude was his biggest drawback and he dropped out of the class.

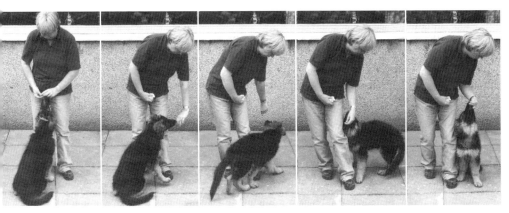

Using titbits with a puppy to achieve 'round to heel'.

Generally, owners are very happy to apply food as an inducement and they feel that they have the answer to successful training. The problem is getting them to realise that food is a means to an end. It is the questioning of an owner on recall problems and suchlike when out for a walk with the dog that brings home the fact that there is more to training than titbits.

Before going any further, it may be advisable to put the various aids into their category of uses. Put simply: Titbits and toys are used as an inducement by means of reward for carrying out an act satisfactorily. That reward encourages the happy and successful participation from the dog in future. The use of titbits can however, play an important role with many dogs, although the discipline and its application can make the difference between 'just feeding a greedy dog' or getting him to be aware that he *must* act in a particular way to receive his treat.

Thought should be given to three important factors:

(a) The type of food for titbits to be used.
(b) The methods of applying titbits.
(c) The exercises or elements for application.

Although dogs will generally react to most forms of titbits, it is the type that generates most interest and enthusiasm that should be used. Dog biscuits are not recommended, they are generally much larger than is necessary and tend to be rather dry. The smaller and tastier the better. The titbits that go over the throat in a single swallow are more likely to maintain the dogs' attention than something he has to break down or chew. There are many good products on the market where the titbits can be broken into suitable sizes. Dried liver cubes or purchased liver treats would probably be voted as the most desirable by the dogs. Although small pieces of cheese or apple can make a dog desperate to please his owner. The important factor is a quick appreciation from the dog for this supplement to the praise and affection from the owner.

The method of applying or the presentation of titbits is as important as the tasty morsels themselves. It should be recognised that dogs cannot see titbits from a distance, but their presentation in a plastic bag or some obvious container can be very effective. A dog can see a plastic bag and can also hear it rustle. The noise of titbits rattling in a container can also be very effective and, with the knowledge that titbits are there for the taking, can be sufficient to bring a dog back when no amount of calling will have any effect.

The actual presentation of the titbits can certainly affect results and it is now preferable to have the dog come in close enough to take the titbit from the owner rather than for the owner to give the dog the titbit. The owner should hold the bag of titbits close to his body (at the dog's nose level if possible) after letting the dog see that they are available. The owner takes a titbit into his clenched hand with palm facing outwards. When the dog comes in and sniffs at the hand, or bag if both hands are together, he opens the hand and lets the dog take his reward.

The clenched hand principle can be utilised at other times, such as with loose-lead walking, but the positioning of the left hand is utilised to draw the dog into the position required by the owner.

There are times when the use of titbits can be most helpful, and others when their use can induce failure unless great care is taken. The use of titbits during the application of active situations can usually help to achieve a happy and responsible performance, with the dog knowing that there is an award to be taken. However, in the case of static situations, or elements of an exercise, the temptation of a titbit can certainly create an unwanted movement. An explanation of active and static situations is described in chapter eleven.

There are exceptions to this general ruling and one common exception is during the retrieve, when a dog is actively holding the article he can make an early drop to create space in his mouth for the expected titbit.

Because of the dangers with 'anticipation of a titbit' it is preferred that training for retrieve and the stay exercises is carried out without titbits or with the greatest care. Play toys can be used instead of titbits. However to give the dog full benefit of fun and games with them as an inducement or reward generally results in a loss of control during the earlier stages of training. The use of toys can result in success if the owner is selective and careful with its application.

Gadgets

DISKS AND THROW CHAINS

These items are used initially to shock the dog into stopping what he is doing, but in a manner that becomes a trigger in the future for the dog to pay attention to the owner's follow up requirement from the dog.

CLICKERS

This gadget is also used as a trigger that is described above, but without the shock treatment.

TOYS

The one thing about the use of toys is that it helps to bring out the best in owner participation. Who can throw a ball or some other item for a dog to catch or chase after without showing the feeling of fun? Such a situation, if used, is to have the toy as the dog's centre of attraction. It should be a well-used inducement to get a dog's attention for the follow up activity. This is one situation when the reward being given immediately after the event is highly successful.

However there are problems that can be associated with the use of toys. If they are used in a training class, they can create a disruptive situation with like-minded beginner dogs waiting their turn. Toys are only of value if the dog is prepared to return with them, otherwise time and the frustrating loss of control will follow. These photographs give examples of suitable toys.

An assortment of useful training toys.

| Sock | Leather | Plastic | Knitted |

In writing about gadgets, my principal comments relate to disks and clickers as they are being pushed as the answer to training and behaviour problems. Before going any further, I shall put the record straight and divulge I do use titbits and toys in training, but have never used disks or clickers although I have used the principles rather more loosely. I hope the explanation that follows will clear me of criticising training techniques I have never used.

I would think that the disks and clickers have been developed from the throw chain that I first read about in the book by Koehler *Guard Dog Training* (1962). The principal features of the throw chain are:

1. It can spread out in flight and has a better chance, than most other objects, of hitting a distracted dog. Some people use a tin can with stones or marbles inside.
2. If the chain misses the dog, the noise of it hitting the ground can be sufficient to generate the dog's attention.
3. When the activity of throwing has become effective, the clink of the chain in the owner's hand is generally sufficient to generate the dog's attention.

The most popular item to be used as a throw chain is the check chain, which has often been used as a collar in the past. It will be thought by some that this approach to controlling a dog is rather crude, but let us look at the use of a set of disks. The demonstrations I have seen with disks have been on television or a video and on each occasion, they have been used in an enclosed area, a consulting room or in the dog's home. In each case, the dog was rather disturbed or frightened during the first few drops of the disks. The dog had nowhere to go, if this had been applied out in the open some of those dogs would probably have run away.

If the throw chain is used at or beside an inattentive but nervous dog out in the open, he would probably run away and it is obvious that the application, if used, should be reserved for suitable situations. I have used it in the past, mainly beside and rarely at the dog. It is just a tool to be used on the right dog at the right time. The appropriate follow up procedure will ensure that the dog has learnt a lesson and will respond in future, eventually with pleasure. It all comes down to the commitment from the person handling the situation. If he is encouraging with his attitude, the dog will respond accordingly. If he is dominant and forceful in his outlook, the dog may respond, but it will not be a happy response.

Hitting a dog bodily with a throw chain will be more of an unpleasant experience than it will hurt. The dog very soon learns to respond to the 'jingle' of the chain, just as he learns to respond to the 'clink' of disks when they hit the floor. There is no reason why a chain cannot be used instead of, and applied, as one would use disks – to have it dropped or thrown in front of a dog, not aiming to hit him.

My last dog was getting on in years and had been out of training for longer than I can remember and last year she was showing her independence. She would sniff when she wanted to sniff and take her own time about responding to my requirements. She was taking advantage of my relaxed attitude to life. Although she had always responded to my whistle better than my voice, I decided to try out the throw chain with her, but not to actually throw it. On this occasion, I gave her a gentle reminder with my voice that she was supposed to be with me, there was no response. As I was right beside her I dropped the chain (not thrown) on her back and her response was immediate. After that the jingle of the chain when I wanted her attention meant she was happy to give it with a look of 'OK Dad, I should have known better'.

Although all my dogs have been taught to respond to the voice and body language, they have also been taught to respond to the whistle, particularly with Send Away, Redirect, Recall, and Stay where you are. With this background, and when helping other people to train their dogs, I have noted that some dogs respond naturally and better to non vocal instructions to carry out a task. However, it is the encouragement from the voice, the body language and the owner's attitude of mind that comes through to the dog and that results in his enthusiastic cooperation, whistle or no whistle.

The use of titbits or toys, clicker, disks or throw chains should not be the first option, but if any of them are felt to be helpful for a particular dog or owner, one or more can be *complementary* to the voice and body language coming from the heart. That is, if you want a dog to be your partner in life.

The change to the conditions that prevail today is now so dramatic, that titbits, toys and gadgets have taken the desired personal commitment out of conditioning for a cooperative canine response. The problem is that when using these training aids to generate canine attention without total owner involvement, does not prepare the dog, or the owner, for more unusual situations when these aids are not at hand. There are so many occasions in real life when a training aid is not at hand and immediate action has become a necessity. The aid may be in a pocket or a belly bag and by the time the aid has been taken out and ready for use it is too late. There are also many situations, when a dog is distracted to the degree that these training aids, with full availability, are of no practical value.

I have already mentioned timing and we should now review the principles. The question is 'What is the correct timing?' There is, in fact, a short space of time when action is of any value; running from the ideal to the latest effective moment. This period of time is very short, and in most cases two or three seconds can be considered too long to be effective. Timing can best be described as:

(a) The time lapse *starts* when the dog is thinking of acting in a particular manner. This is the ideal and most effective time to act.

(b) The period *finishes* as the dog is completing the particular action. This is the very latest that an owner has to affect a dog's actions.

The ideal through to latest effective moment is the 'owner response time'. The effectiveness of human reaction can therefore be said to be in relation to the timing. The most effective reaction to an owner's intervention would take place during the canine thinking period. If an owner is sufficiently observant, he can realise when his dog is thinking of acting in a particular manner. In fact, on many of these occasions, past experience should warn an owner of the developing situations. This applies to unwanted actions an owner wishes to eradicate and to desirable actions an owner wishes to consolidate. Anticipation is the name of the game and the owner's ability to respond within the appropriate response time will make the difference between success and failure.

I will give an example of this. While out for a walk with a dog the sight of another dog relatively close may cause an aggressive reaction. If the owner sees the other dog first, he can observe his dog's initial reaction to the other dog's presence. This knowledge can give an owner the opportunity to take preventive action and divert his dog's attention before his own dog has decided to show an unwanted or unpleasant side of his nature. Strong and urgent deflecting action on the owner's part, while the dog is thinking, would be most appropriate. If an owner waits until his own dog has shown this unwanted or unpleasant side of his nature, he may or may not be able to stop his dog. Just as important, he is less likely to teach the dog self control. Every action an owner takes should, if possible, be carried out in a manner that will help to prevent a recurrence of his dog's unwanted response.

It is understandable why so many owners do not appreciate the importance of timing, when I see that so many instructors and behaviourists fail to bring the point home. I have watched so many television programmes involving behaviourists when they have applied disks, clickers and the like to affect a dog's reaction, and they may be able to apply them with perfect timing, but I have yet to hear them explain to the dog owner the absolute importance of this timing. It has been the same with training classes where titbits are utilised as an inducement. All too often there is little or no importance conveyed to the owners of timing – of the effect of good timing and the ineffectiveness of bad timing.

To make matters worse the titbits, toys and attention generating gadgets are used instead of, or without sufficient involvement of the owner. As previously described, all too often, there is insufficient personal commitment to have the owner sufficiently effective when these artificial inducements are not immediately available.

I have no complaint against the use of them and will only recommend the use of these aids if they are to be complementary to the full commitment of the dog's owner. A fuller application of titbits and toys will be illustrated during the application of training techniques.

Principal control equipment and additional training aids

The choice and variety of equipment can play a significant part in an owner's ability to achieve success with his dog in training. These details are added to this chapter because it is considered that they play a very important part in the application of inducements or incentives. Although collars and leads are the principal pieces of equipment there are other items that should be given consideration. They are grouped as:

1. Various types of collar.
2. Suitable leads.
3. Trailing lines and activity cords.

The owner should understand the principles and application of control equipment so that the greatest value can be achieved from the chosen items. The various combinations of equipment utilised have three basic functions:

1. As the principal controlling aid for training. Apart from giving the owner confidence that he can handle a situation and that the application of these items will help to convince the dog that it is in his best interest to cooperate.
2. As an effective measure of restraint when situations develop that could go beyond the control of the owner and the dog.
3. As a controlling factor to be utilised when the owner is not in a position to give the dog his full attention.

Although the three basic functions have just been given, the choice of equipment is generally governed by the requirements of (1) control for training.

COLLARS

The choice of collar can play a significant part in the owner's ability to control his dog, although generally speaking it is the application of both collar and lead or line which controls the effectiveness of an owner's actions.

Unless in the hands of an expert, the conventional *buckle* type of collar has little effect on an owner's ability to control his dog and is not generally recommended.

Check collars come in a variety of styles with the most commonly used in the past being known as the *check chain*. The problem with the metal linked chain type is its ability to cut away at the hairs around the dog's neck every time tension is applied; the small link chains do most damage. Check collars are also made of leather, flat or round, nylon webbing or rope and often they are just a matter of choice, which is preferred for the job in hand.

These check collars should be chosen to suit the size of the dog and ideally should just be able to slip over the dog's head with little to spare. An overlong check collar round a dog's neck may affect an owner's application of collar and lead; it can also fall off and get lost or it can get caught up with something that could create a dangerous situation.

With a properly fitting check collar a short but sharp jerk on the lead should gain the dog's attention to terminate an uncontrolled situation or in preparation for a more attentive and constructive period. It is important that this type of collar is put over the dog's head in the correct manner. With the dog at the handler's left side the collar is worn in such a manner that it will automatically slacken off when any tension is released. *Note:* The use of check chains has become much less common, but I believe the instruction on use should still be made available. The *combi-collar* is a much more popular piece of equipment.

The *combi-collar* is an excellent alternative to the check collar. This style has a short chain loop that is attached to a webbing band and is adjustable. The collar is easily adjusted to slip neatly over the dog's head and, in action,

Selection of collars.

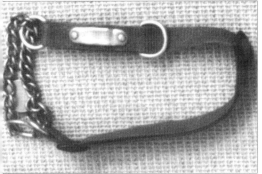

Check chain.

Combi-collar.

Rope check.

it has a limited amount of slip. It is a convenient and effective collar for training and also general use.

The *halti* or *dogalter* and similar types of head harness is another concept that has been introduced to the techniques of canine control. This form of harness can be used in conjunction with a collar or on its own. Control is applied with the lead attached to a ring under the dog's lower jaw. It is a most effective form of control and is particularly useful for owners who find it difficult to control their dogs. As the *halti* was the first of its kind on the market this now seems to be the common expression for such equipment and any further reference will be to a *halti*.

Modern special body harnesses are now available to help ensure that dog walking can be a pleasure instead of a continued battle between dog and owner.

These harnesses create canine discomfort when they try to pull, and most dogs learn very quickly to respect such equipment. The harness recommended by Dr Roger Mugford is called the *lupi* and I have found it to be a helpful alternative to the *halti* for people in difficulty.

Leads

A good strong lead with a dependable clip attachment is essential. I have found the length of about four feet to be ideal for training and normal handling practices, although a forty inch lead seems to have become the standard length. Leads shorter than this do not give the owner room to manoeuvre for preventive or corrective action and longer leads can become difficult to handle.

Although a good quality leather lead is ideal, the use of soft nylon or cotton webbing can be equally suitable. Chain leads are very hard on the hands of an owner and make it difficult for him to apply proper control techniques and should, therefore, be avoided.

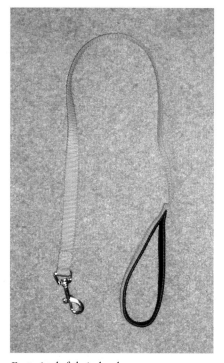

Forty-inch fabric lead.

Flexi-leads that automatically retract have a length of up to twenty-five feet and can be of value in training for canine control. The flexi-lead can be locked, if desired, at any length to suit the situation or it can be allowed to run out or in at will.

This type of lead is not easily handled for training for loose lead walking and it is not recommended for this purpose. It can be utilised for testing the effect of loose-lead walking training where complete freedom is given to the flexi movement. The dog knows he is attached, but the owner also knows that movement and verbal actions are required on his part to control the situation, rather than tugs on the lead.

The flexi-lead, however, has greater uses when applied instead of lines of various lengths and this will be discussed in the next section.

TRAILING LINES AND ACTIVITY CORDS

With many dogs, dragging the trailing line is an inhibiting factor and great use can be made of this means of control in training. Although lines can be of any length there are certain lengths that are ideally suited to particular purposes or to counter certain canine reactions.

The most suitable lines are made of nylon cord and of a size that has a listed breaking strain of approximately 700 lb (318 kg). Lengths or reels of this cord can be purchased from ironmongers, DIY stores and some sports shops. On these trailing lines it is advisable to attach a trigger clip of the type that is used on the end of standard leads. When required, a holding loop can be tied on the other end of the long line.

Suitable lines and applications using this approach are as follows:

- A thirty-foot trailing line with a trigger clip at one end and a loop at the other can be used as dragging line for dogs that will not come back when called.
- A six-foot trailing line with a trigger clip at one end can be utilised instead of the thirty-foot line or to replace it before giving the dog greater freedom. This line can also be used indoors, where there are

Selection of lines and cords.

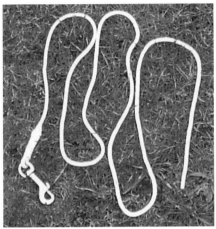

Six feet trailing line.

Six feet activity cord.

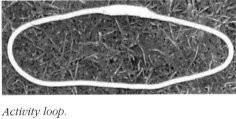

Activity loop.

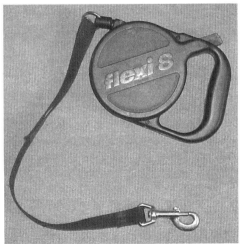

Thirty feet trailing line.

Flexi-lead.

no knots or attachments that can catch under doors, etc. *Note:* This line can be used to replace the Activity cord.

- The six-foot Activity cord has a loop at one end and the other end is free of knots or attachments. This can be used through the ring of the collar instead of the lead. When training the dog the cord can be allowed to slip out without the dog realising he is free.
- The Activity loop takes up about twenty to twenty-four inches of cord and should be attached to the collar to hold as and when required. The cord can then be released from the hand when the dog is being let loose to carry out a planned activity.
- A flexi-lead can be used for getting attention and countering recall behaviour problems to give some distance between dog and owner. The flexi-lead would be utilised in the same way as the lead for attention generating and the flexi-lead will automatically retract as the dog returns. However, the owner does not have quite the same freedom to use both hands for encouragement, or to achieve a balanced welcome.

The use or abuse of this equipment will be discussed during the application of training techniques.

Chapter 8

A FULLER UNDERSTANDING

To stamp your authority on the relationship with your dog is a target worth achieving. Without that authority, the dog becomes the master or pack leader and a liability. However, this does not mean the use of harsh treatment or prolonged use of the collar and lead. These practices, especially when applied with malice, anger and brutality will certainly ruin a relationship.

There is no doubt that the owner's voice plus body language are the most powerful ingredients he has to cement a good relationship with his canine friends. However, use of the voice and accompanying body language should be applied in a manner to suit the occasion.

There should never be a problem in coordinating the vocal approach with body language, it is such a natural combination to have the voice giving the same message as the body. It takes great and unnecessary effort to have voice and body movements in conflict; it is not natural and serves no useful purpose.

It can be difficult for some owners to use their voices in a manner that suits the occasion. With some, it is difficult to remove harshness from their voices and with others it is just as difficult to have them use a more firm tone of voice when it is required. I have always said that what comes out of the mouth should come from the heart. If it is an occasion for a soft and encouraging tone of voice, it should sound that way to the dog. If the situation requires a demanding approach, that is how it should sound to the dog. The variations in between should again be adjusted to suit the situation.

The beauty of the voice is that it can be applied immediately and instantly changed to suit the ever-changing conditions. It can also be difficult at times to have owners use titbits in an effective way, or to apply disks or clickers with any degree of satisfaction. When attending Obedience or Working trials training sessions or just watching dog owners exercising their dogs in the park the use of titbits is quite obvious, but seldom with their correct application. I have yet to see or hear disks or clickers in use. I wonder why? The use of the voice is very prominent, but in so many cases, it is the incorrect use of it that is so significant.

To my mind, much greater effort should be put into the timing and use of voice control and with the application of other inducements to be used, but only when they are found to have an advantage.

The beauty of the voice is that it can be applied spontaneously under any condition and with unlimited variations. An owner is much less likely to be caught unprepared if the voice is the first choice for stopping a dog from acting in a manner that does not suit him. The voice should also be the first choice along with body language for encouraging a dog to continue doing something that is to the benefit of the owner, and obviously to the dog.

For example, if a dog is thinking or actually sniffing at a street lamp, a hit with the voice is the most natural way of preventing or terminating the act if it is considered to be undesirable. Although there can be advantages with the use of a set of disks or a clicker, these advantages are outweighed by the spontaneity or variations from the use of the voice. The use of titbits would be a useful addition to praise (but not instead of), when the dog has reacted in a satisfactory manner. If the dog is going to pick up a piece of stick and the owner wants to encourage retrieving, again the voice is the most natural way of supporting and promoting his dog's action.

The use of vocal cords, unless distance, wind direction or frailty of voice causes problems, is the most natural approach to working with a dog. Unfortunately, many owners do not seem to be able to vary the application of the voice to suit the occasion. In situations affected by the lack of voice projection, an owner whose training involved a whistle as an alternative will realise the benefit. I recall one client who had a problem getting her dog's attention when out for a walk, no doubt she had the same problem at home where it would not be so apparent or perhaps so important. I gave her advice on how to use her vocal cords and I demonstrated what to do by practical application when her dog ignored her 'gentle' approach.

The husband was out with this lady and me, when I was unsuccessfully trying to get her to apply the appropriate deflections of voice. Her husband shouted to her, 'Why don't you speak to that dog the way you speak to me when you want something done'. He had hit the nail right on the head; there was no 'punch' in her voice to generate the attention she wanted when she spoke to the dog. As far as the dog was concerned, the owner did not mean what she said. However, from experience the husband knew the score.

The effect is the same with some owners in the competitive field of work. I have seen it often in training and competition, especially when the fullest of co-operation is required from the dog. Readers should note that as it is a different world, the pet dog owner may think it is not important to get the fullest of co-operation, but this thinking would be wrong. It is just as important within many domestic situations to apply strict control, such as wanting a dog to come back when called.

With any of the agility exercises, the maximum of output is required from a dog and yet there are owners who give a half-hearted instruction for the dog to jump. Little commitment from the owner results in a similar return from the dog. Thinking back to this client and her husband situation, she knew how to generate the attention of her husband, but would not apply the same commitment to her dog. Dogs can take the sharpest and shortest of vocal blasts so long as this is immediately followed through with gentle and encouraging tones. The vocal blast is to gain attention and the follow through is to achieve a willing and happy reaction required from the dog.

Quite recently, I was involved in a situation that highlighted a typical action from a domestic dog owner. I was in the park exercising my GSD and she had her ball in her mouth when a young Cocker Spaniel came running up to her. Ceilidh dropped her ball to give full attention to this little whipper snapper. There was no aggravation from either dog and after they were allowed to investigate each other, I told Ceilidh to go and pick up her ball so that we could get on our way. The little spaniel was going to follow her and the owner called him back. After a couple of calls, the dog returned to his mistress – good, no problem there. However, when the dog returned she stretched out her arm to full extension and gave the little dog a titbit, but not a word of appreciation or request to stay. After taking the titbit, the dog immediately turned and ran back to Ceilidh. What a waste of effort with a good little dog, but I think that readers will be able to see that mistakes were made.

It is also the timing of the owner's action along with the variation of voice and body language that generates a worthy canine response. Barbara Woodhouse has been criticised by many for her approach to dog training. Whatever failings, and she did have some, she had timing to perfection and her success with a dog was principally due to her ability to time her actions.

I often feel that being self-conscious affects many an owner's approach to his dog and I have used the following expression to many a class of dog owners, 'You do not have to be daft to handle a dog – but it does help.'

When I started with my first dog, I was consciously wondering what people would think of my efforts. During the earliest days at a training club, I watched as people went on the floor to train for an individual exercise, such as recall or retrieve. I thought to myself, I can get on to the floor to do the group exercises, heelwork and stays, but I have no confidence to get up with a dog and do the individual stuff. It did not take me long to change and, before I realised it, I was up there concentrating on recalls and retrieves. When I get an owner to think about his dog rather than how people see him as an individual, the chances of success are on the positive side of the scales.

At one stage I was going to say that women were worse than men at applying their voices, but so many men let the gender down by their macho approach to communicating and demanding from their dogs. Both sexes have a lot to learn.

Most canine behaviour or training problems are based on the owners' inability to apply the appropriate vocal and body language with their dogs. Titbits can be a good back up – as an 'as well as' and there are occasions when gadgets may be of good value. In exceptional circumstances, or for a particular reason, gadgets can be utilised to complement the full involvement of the owner.

Instructors and behaviourists should put much more emphasis on involvement and contribution from their clients by means of body language and vocal encouragement, instead of filling their heads with specialised gadgets that most of them will never be able to use properly.

The use and timing of your dog's name is another factor that is extremely important, but this will be fully discussed during the application of training techniques.

Chapter 9

SAFETY AND RELIABILITY

Safety and reliability are factors that can go together. Where there is reliability in a dog's responses, safety is generally assured. That assurance is greater when an owner fully appreciates that any liberties taken by a dog can generally lead to disobedience and thereby deterioration in the safety factor.

Even without taking the safety factor into consideration, reliability helps to cement the performances from the dog, and therefore the relationship between owner and dog. There is nothing more pleasing than having a dog respond to an owner's just requirements. It is a great feeling of achievement when an owner knows and respects his dog's ability to answer the request he understands, and has the trained ability to respond satisfactorily.

Safety in itself is a valid subject to be discussed, particularly where accusations of canine interference into the lives of others can cause unpleasantness at the least, or at worst a court case for unruly behaviour that brings owner and dog into disrepute.

A lot has been written about the Dangerous Dog Act and there is no doubt that those of us who have read the canine press, are fully aware of the implications of owning a dog that may cause some distress to a member of the community. The accusation of distress may be real, it may be from somebody who has a phobia or is paranoiac about the presence of a dog and may imagine his distress. Whatever the circumstances, the threat is always there.

Speaking to the pet owning public, I find that the Dangerous Dog Act has little meaning to most of them and it can be difficult to engender real concern and appreciation of the dangers. I have been involved as an expert witness defending dogs in a number of court cases and have found that very few owners consider that their dogs could ever be classed as dangerous in any way. Yet, there are many occurrences where the absence of simple precautions or consideration for others does lead to a situation where a dog does become a nuisance and causes annoyance or stress to some members of the public. That annoyance may even be fun to the dog, but can easily be interpreted as an intended attack.

There are so many instances where simple canine activities are annoying to members of the public. Dogs running uncontrolled can ruin children's play games and have them running scared – a recipe for disaster. All too often I have had to ask a dog owner to get his dog under control when that dog was pestering my own dogs, while they were on the lead. Many an unpleasant and potentially dangerous situation has developed because dog owners feel that their dogs have the right to uncontrolled freedom. During my forty plus years as a German Shepherd Dog owner my dogs, whilst under full control either on the lead or being held by the collar, have been physically attacked on nine different occasions and by a variety of dogs. None of these attacking dogs was remotely recognisable as one of the so-called guarding breeds. The owners of these dogs had not given a single thought to the dangerous situation that their dogs were creating. Safety and consideration never seems to enter their minds.

Life is built round safety precautions, in the home, in the work place and out in the street. Neglect safety and accidents are more likely to happen. It may be said that there is no such thing as an accident; every incident of this nature can be due to a lack of knowledge, experience, foresight or care. We all have accidents of some sort, and an objective analysis of each event would indicate that somebody, somewhere, lacked the knowledge, experience, foresight or care. Dog ownership is just one aspect of life where accidents occur for the same reasons as in all life's chapters.

There are many bodies who work hard to create and ensure that safety standards are of the highest order, but in the world of dogs the word 'safety' is seldom, if ever, written about. If not written, it is unlikely to be a principle topic of conversation. We read plenty about the Dangerous Dog Act and its effects on dog owners. However, the prevention of situations, which could warrant the application of the Act never seem to get a mention. I am sure that most training instructors and behaviourists are working for an accident-free canine population in every day life, but is the freedom from danger and risks in the forefront of their consideration for training or correction activities?

Reliability must be considered as a prime constituent of safety. Full reliability is the assurance that a dog will always act or respond in a prescribed manner, no matter what conditions prevail. The owner is always in control. This may be asking for the impossible, but an owner's appreciation of the degree of reliability expected under stressful conditions can help assure that foresight will ensure the implementation of preventive or avoidance measures.

As an example – if an owner realises that he has limited control over his dog when off the lead, and he knows from past experience that the dog is likely to chase others dogs, running children, cyclists or joggers, the owner has a choice. Keep the dog on the lead or when free be particularly observant and put the dog into a controlled situation when any of these distractive activities become evident; and before the dog has time to react in an undesirable manner. There are, of course, other alternatives if the owner has the knowledge or is suitably advised.

Training instructors and behaviourists all have their own individual attitudes towards problem correction, but all too often safety from day one is not given sufficient prominence. Dogs that chase or show aggression, dogs that pull on the lead in a manner that creates a danger to the owner or to the general public, all have owners who want and need immediate relief from these undesirable canine activities. Long term conditioning or retraining is important, but the lack of immediate relief causes stress to all concerned and safety can become the first casualty.

The medical profession have long since recognised the need for immediate relief from the symptoms of health problems. Patients expect, and doctors are happy to prescribe, drugs and supports or the like to alleviate pain or discomfort. The cure can require a completely different course of action and involve a longer-term approach. Even when cures are not available for particular health problems immediate and long-term relief remedies are still made available; the patient more than welcomes them.

Dog owners are also entitled to the same consideration where behaviour problems are ruining an otherwise happy companionship. Any assistance to overcome problems should contain the following considerations.

- An immediate relief programme
- Long term programme of correction
- The influence of an immediate relief programme on long-term correction activities.
- Consideration of side effects of either programme
- The measure of safety built into the programme

We should look at the two most common problems that affect dog owners, and consider these every day situations:

1. Dogs that do not come back when called.
2. Dogs pulling on leads.

Dogs that do not come back when called

All too often, we hear of training classes that concentrate on recall training as applied in the competitive field, but without other advice being given. We also hear of behaviourists who recommend the use of toys or titbits to induce a dog back, but with little else to induce success

There are a number of thoughtful experts who will advocate the use of both safety and reliability measures. However, these experts also advise on the need to prevent circumstances from arising where the dog can be in full control of the situation. This is the key to success. Every time a dog is in a position to defy the owner's requirements the possibility of achieving a reliable response diminishes. The level of safety is matched to the degree of reliability.

It is the advice on how to achieve a measure of freedom, and yet be in control, that is most helpful to owners while they carry out the longer, more purposeful correction training.

Dogs pulling on the lead

The general approach at a training class doing group heelwork in a hall does not appear to be of much value. The dog may walk to heel during a training session, then pull the owner out of the hall and along the street on completion of the evening's work. Advice is often given to use toys or titbits as an inducement to stay at heel and that can work for a competitive approach to heel work. However, it is generally useless for relaxed loose lead walking, unless other remedies are introduced for a casual walk to the shops or an exercise area. Toys cannot be used effectively for the majority of people while out for a walk. Titbits can be useful, but by such feeding, the dog has had so much that his weight increase slows his pace down.

An owner requires advice and demonstrations on how to take a relaxed walk without having to pit his strength against that of his dog. I do not claim that the dog is going to enjoy many of these remedies, but most of them do create varying degrees of unpleasantness from their owners. A dog has no entitlement to make his owner's life a misery and, the sooner preventive and corrective action becomes effective, the quicker full harmony returns to the canine/owner relationship.

Safety covers all aspects of canine life and there could be a never-ending debate on the subject, but at the end of the day, it all comes down to consideration and control. Consideration for other members of the community. How often have we heard 'He just wants to play' – 'If you let your dog free they can socialise, my dog won't fight'. You will normally find that the dog owners who make those comments have no control over their dogs and it only requires one uncontrolled dog in a pair to create an unsafe situation. Consideration and control cannot be separated, they equate with safety and reliability.

Predictability and perception

Predictability and perception are very much involved in the reliability scene. If we can predict how a dog is going to act or react, we can be mentally prepared to encourage or discourage the relevant situations.

Firstly, it is important to understand how predictable our dogs are and how perceptive the dog owners have to become. Dogs are predictable to situations that repeat themselves; the problem is that, the conditions surrounding these situations are not always the same.

We find that 'fair weather' training owners who enter the field of competition often find difficulties (or failures) when they are expected to perform during rain, thunder or snow. They have not trained for it.

To help understand predictability, I would put situations into one of three different categories.

1. Situation where a dog will definitely respond satisfactorily to the owner's requirements.
2. A grey area of doubt where the owner's perception of the situation is unclear and the dog's response is in doubt.
3. Situations where the dog's response is highly unlikely to be satisfactory.

When a dog fails to respond constructively to a naturally expected situation, do not blame the dog, but look for the deviation from the norm, analyse for a course of action, then create the conditions that will give assured satisfaction.

Chapter 10

UNDERSTANDING ASSORTED FACTORS

There are a number of factors, which are important in themselves, but do not warrant individual chapters, and they are now put together in a manner that should be meaningful to the reader.

Stress (Tension)

Stress is part of our daily lives – whether we like it or not. To some extent, it is the same with our dogs; stress is a factor that affects them as well. That tension may be minor in nature and well handled by the dogs, but stress under certain conditions can make life very difficult for the domestic pet, the trained competitive or professional working dog. It can also be a critical factor that may affect the reliability expected from your dog.

In my book, *Your Dog – A Guide To Solving Behaviour Problems* there is a full case study of a behaviour situation relating to stressful dogs that do not like to be left alone. This study includes preventive and corrective measures.

There are situations in the field of constructive training where stress can and does ruin performances. Fortunately, most behaviour or training problems caused by stress are avoidable, although there are dogs with inherited weaknesses that cause stress in most situations that are new to them; this will always create difficulties. Most dogs with these problems have their present or previous owners or their breeding to blame for their stressful reactions.

The prevention of most stressful situations is relatively easy; it is the later correction if allowed to develop, which requires much more patience.

It is our function to apply the correct approach to stress during the early development of situations. This may mean the deliberate creation of the correct amount of stress when required, then to control the situation in a manner that alleviates that stress. The dog accepts controlled repeats of these situations at a later time. Eventually the situation seems natural to the dog and can then be taken in his stride.

An ideal example is that of teaching a dog to sit and stay sitting (similar with down and stay). Most dogs that break the stay in training for domestic, competitive or professional purposes do so for one of two reasons.

1. They are too stressed or confused and will want to get back to their owner.

2. There is a lack of canine responsibility due to the manner in which he has been trained.

In both of these cases, it is likely that there was a failure to utilise and manage stress levels during the earliest stages of training. The application of stress and its control will be fully discussed during the application of training techniques.

Physical and mental maturity

It is so easy for an owner to start training on some aspect within his requirements before the dog is suitably developed. This does not happen so much on the physical side of development, unless agility is within the programme. Some dogs will physically mature quicker than others, but whatever programme has been developed it is better to take guidance from the knowledgeable people within your breed or activity.

Although the same can be said about mental maturity, the variance within any breed can be wider than would be expected. It was said many years ago that training should not start until a youngster was six months old, and this may still hold today. Unfortunately, this thinking was taken to mean what it said and, in too many cases, puppies were put under no restraints or measures of control until that six-month period was up. The problem was then to achieve control over youngsters who had received no measure of discipline.

Gentle conditioning on basic training requirements during those early months, and being properly carried out, can make life much easier for an owner. It also prepares the youngsters for the life to come.

Early stage training should cover the need to pay attention to the owner when it is called for. Without that attention, nothing can be achieved. An eight to ten-week-old puppy can and should respond to this level of training, and to know the pleasures of that response. Preventing a puppy from jumping up from day one (in his new home), be it on people or furniture is best achieved before the habit has had a chance to appear.

A good guide with pups, from about six months of age, is to train initially on the exercises that come naturally to the individual pup. Recalling is an ideal exercise (not necessarily with a stay and to the competitive exercise requirements) from any distance and with a variety of distractions; this is a good start and the foundation for a successful future.

Loose lead walking is another exercise to consider from the day a collar and lead are applied, the German Shepherd pup, illustrated overleaf, pulling on the lead is no problem, but will be if not corrected before he has the strength to take full control. We should recognise that training for competitive heel work at an early age can be counter productive. That level of concentration can be beyond the capacity of youngsters with a butterfly mind. Some dogs can be a year old before they are ready to concentrate on

A puppy which pulls can become a difficult adult.

serious heelwork. These same dogs can apply great concentration on working a track for some fifteen minutes or longer, because it is something they love to do.

It is often the case that owners can make good use of a youngster's natural ability to being trained and give him (and the owner) confidence before thinking of serious training in the exercises that appear to be more demanding from both of them.

There is at least one exercise I would exempt from these delays and that is training for the stay exercises, particularly the sit stay. Provided this exercise is trained properly, it gives a youngster a sense of responsibility that will carry him through the rest of his life.

Conflicts of interest

Conflicts of interest are an unpleasant fact and as human beings we all have to deal with them. Our dogs will always be attracted to a distraction unless they are trained to be selective in what takes their attention. They will also be required to respond immediately there is a request or demand to maintain attention on their owners during times of temptation to view some interesting diversion.

The ease or difficulty in countering a distraction depends on the degree of conflict, also the dog's assessment of his need to cooperate with his owner at that particular moment.

It is very important that an owner has the ability to recognise when conflict of interest does exist, and is too great to achieve success under the prevailing conditions. It is therefore the owner's responsibility to recognise that any failure is his to bear for not recognising the development of the unwanted situation. Success however is there for the taking, if the owner has the ability to change the situation so that success can be assured.

Remembering that the dog will always do what he considers to be in his best interest at that moment in time, it is the ever-changing conditions that determine the dog's interest in some deviation from the norm.

As an example, the distance between dog and owner can influence a dog's response, and this will vary from one dog to another. The greater the distance between dog and owner the more the dog can feel he has complete independence, he is out of 'controlling' distance' and may not respond favourably towards his owner's wishes. However, the dog may be worried when he realises there is an unusually great distance between them and he will make a hasty return.

Separation, or distance between dog and owner is of greater importance than many owners appreciate and this should be given serious consideration when there is reason to worry about the apparent inconsistencies in a dog's response.

Success or even a minor success is always better than a failure – there is no such thing as a minor failure. Any failure of a dog to meet the owner's requirements will always affect the future. So many times I have heard a disgruntled owner say 'he has never done that before' without them realising there has been a change in conditions that has contributed to the failure in question.

The same can be said for a dog acting in the owner's favour without the owner realising it was an unforeseen change that brought out the unexpected success.

The reasons for these unexpected failures or successes are not usually understood and are likely to continue under similar conditions and failures can develop where success has been a norm in the past. We would be so lucky if unforeseen successes continued without the appreciation of the reason for the change.

When owners say 'he has never done that before' they generally think it is a 'one off' and do nothing about it. Before long they will find that 'one off' has become a habit and one that is difficult to change

Avoidance

To avoid situations that create difficulties for an owner may well be termed as a defeatist attitude. There are certain times when a problem must be faced head on and be handled in the most positive manner. However, there are times when some situations should be avoided until conditioning or training has countered the unwanted tendencies. With young dogs avoidance until maturity can, on occasions, be nature's cure.

It should be recognised that every time there is a lapse and the dog has the opportunity to indulge in some unwanted behaviour, progress to its elimination would be hampered. This will nullify much of the hard work being put in to correct such situations.

An example of avoidance can cover a dog that chases joggers, children, and the like. A lot of work can go into recall training with distractions and avoidance of opportunities to undisciplined chasing and yet, one slip up of freedom can badly interrupt such a programme. It may mean starting from scratch again – it can be very frustrating.

The alternative or addition to avoidance that can be very helpful in overcoming undesirable situations is that of deflecting a dog's attention. To do this you create a suitable distraction prior to or as the dog realises he can act in an undesirable manner. This deflecting activity must be carried out in a manner that will give the dog great pleasure for the period of time that is necessary.

One approach would be applying owner's backward movement, on or off the lead, and drawing the dog's attention with great excitement is important. Ball, toy play or the use of titbits, if suited to the occasion, may also be the answer. Whatever approach is applied, it must be well worthwhile for the dog. This may be termed as creating a 'pre-occupation' to prevent the dog from appreciating there is a distraction at hand that could cause difficulties for the owner.

I recall one of my dogs when I applied such a practice would look and see what the distraction was, then he would immediately return to me, or if asked to, he would stay where he was. He had no intention of disobeying my instructions, but from my tone of voice, he knew there was a reason for them.

There are times when an aversion requires to be applied with accurate and immediate timing to be effective. On many occasions, a sharp and strongly given 'No' can be sufficient to stop a dog in his tracks. However, this or any other unpleasant interruption in a dog's activities must, when achieved, be changed to a follow up activity with a show of great appreciation for his cooperation.

The application of these activities is a matter of choice and to suit the particular situation. There will always be one option that is likely to make success easier than the others.

Getting it wrong

I think in my lifetime with dogs I have seen, known of, or contributed to most of the mistakes that are made in the conditioning or training of dogs for domestic, competitive or professional purposes.

I think the biggest problem is that some dogs seem to soak up undesirable practices and still have a measure of success. They may not be very happy, but the fact that the owners are satisfied with their performances gives these owners the confidence to go forward as good and experienced instructors. When these owners take on the responsibility of becoming instructors, they pass on the methods they consider to be sound. All too often, sound basics do not seem to be relevant.

To carry out an analysis of problems we must look at the causes. There may not be a single cause, but these causes can generally be put into one of two categories:

1. An inappropriate approach to training.
2. Inappropriate timing, owner attitude or types of reward – even the dreaded punishment.

Lack of canine responsibility can be part of the problem and this is generally the result of the owner's 'lack of positive commitment' to the situation. It can result in canine confusion and, because of this, many dogs fail to understand what is wanted of them at 'that particular moment in time'.

Stress – confusion – uncertainty can give the impression of downright disobedience. The dog suffers, the owner becomes exasperated and the instructor thinks he has a 'right pair' on his hands. All the time he can be applying the wrong approach for that particular partnership.

Recognition of skills

To help focus on the need for dog training and the value of a properly structured approach to the subject, the following questions should be examined.

Why train dogs?
Why do owners require particular skills?
Who can help attain these skills?

Why train dogs?

Good enjoyable canine companionship can only come from a well-behaved dog, a dog that knows his place in the structure of his family and is happy to accept a controlled domestic, competitive or professional environment.

To obtain a controlled but enjoyable companionship for the dog, the owner, the family and the community at large, the dog must receive a certain measure of training. For the competitive or professionally handled dog a sound training is required in the basic exercises before the advanced work can begin.

This training may be in the form of educating the dog through the experiences of life to prevent him becoming an embarrassment. On the other hand, structured training may also be required to prevent or correct undesirable situations from developing.

With the family dog being such a common feature of our lives, canine behaviour has now become a factor that cannot be ignored. The need to have owners educate and train their dogs to fit into the community is now a moral necessity.

Why do owners require particular skills?

Daily situations that develop within the community make it clear that a proportion of dog owners do not understand or appreciate the effect it has when their dog's behaviour is uncontrolled. Other owners do appreciate the effect of independent and undesirable canine activities, but they do not have the knowledge or ability to create conditions that would prevent embarrassing canine situations

To achieve the necessary understanding, knowledge and ability to control their dogs, owners do require a variety of skills to achieve that objective.

Who can help attain these skills?

There are many books on the subject in the marketplace. They are designed to help owners develop the skills required to achieve a well-controlled dog. In many instances the appropriate book is sufficient to give the owner the knowledge and the ability to achieve the desired control over his canine companion and also to develop into the world of competitive or professional work. Quite often owners require the personal touch, they require the capability of an expert in this specialised field to give them the knowledge and expertise to achieve the desired results. However the more the owner understands from sound reading material the more he can understand an instructor's requirements or can manage without such external help.

There are many training clubs or independent organisations throughout the country that are available with instructors who are prepared to share their knowledge and ability. So long as that knowledge and ability is sound, their work can be of great value within the dog training community.

LEARNING FROM OTHER DISCIPLINES

Within any discipline of training there is a tendency to concentrate on tried and tested methods within that discipline. There has been and still are enterprising people who look into methods employed in other disciplines and adopt the new method in a manner that suits their own training environment.

We can take the excellent methods utilised in training Guide Dogs, but must remember the hours of hard work that is being applied by specially trained personnel, and with specially selected dogs. Not every dog makes the grade. Horse whisperers brought out a great interest in the method being used, but few seemed to have been able to make use of (or understand) the approach being applied.

Working through my life within the field of Obedience, Working trials and Behaviour Management has helped me assess the difference in approaches for each of these three disciplines. I have also looked outside these fields of activity for other methods that could be of value and have found that there are techniques that could be employed within certain aspects of training.

It was in the 1970s when I attended an industrial seminar on solving manufacturing problems that I came away with ideas that did help in the work place and could also be useful in the field of dog training. The most important innovations that changed my outlook in dog training involved the following:

- To look at the opposite to the standard practices. This also involved examining the extremes of situations.
- The application of a matrix to help understand the nature of a potential problem.

It may be noted in Chapter 13 that Generating Attention with the prominence of backward movement has replaced heelwork and recall at the earliest stages of training. It is much easier to keep a dog's attention while the owner is moving backwards with the dog following.

Most of the sit and stay training is carried out immediately behind the dog (straddled) instead of in front. It is much easier to maintain a sit stay from immediately behind the dog.

Praise is heaped on the dog from day one instead of the command and silence usually demanded – in case the dog moved. A dog that can be praised when left at the stay is much more secure than one that is not.

In the section relating to Retrieve, training describes the application of a matrix to help people understand why dogs do not always do what is expected of them.

Each of these methods came out of an industrial environment and I have found that they have an important place in the field of dog training.

Much of the material that helps with the skills for training has been included in Part One. Part Two continues by giving the details required for Objectives, Methods and Techniques.

PART 2

Chapter 11

INTRODUCING TRAINING ROUTINES

Managing objectives

Whatever we do in life, it should be worthwhile and clear in our minds. These objectives may change with an increase of knowledge and ability, but the objectives should be the driving force behind the efforts to be expended. Dog training or behaviour management is part of that philosophy.

There was a time when most people who bought a puppy or an older dog did so for companionship and without the knowledge that there was such a thing as dog training clubs; canine behaviourists had not been invented. All too often that companionship was spoilt because of behaviour or control problems. With luck there may have been a dog training club in their area and with more luck owners found out about them.

With some owners the objective became 'owning a well behaved dog' and with others, their success and the knowledge that competitions were available made a difference; the objectives rose to a higher level.

Success was and is the achieving of the objectives the owners set for themselves.

Training objectives

Where there are behaviour problems, the objectives may be easy to understand, but achieving results can well be another matter. However, like training for the basics of control, or more advanced exercises (objectives), each stage or intermediate target becomes an objective in itself, and can be taken in conjunction with any other problem or training objective being planned. For example, a dog that does not come back when called and is also an escapee from a garden should have both problems taken into account. Also in basic training the 'recall' and 'sit' or 'down stay' may seem to be completely separate exercises, but the methods of training should be coordinated to ensure that one does not create unexpected problems for the other.

With this in mind, each training exercise should be broken down into *elements*, and if need be, into *sub elements*. This will ensure that the training of such elements can be examined for the most suitable methods and techniques to be used, or be modified to suit the circumstances.

To clarify the situation the full range of basic training exercises will be used to demonstrate the general approach.

Basic training exercises

- Heelwork (Domestic – Loose Lead Walking)
- Recall (Domestic – Come Back When Called)
- Sit Stay
- Down Stay
- Stand Stay
- Although some would consider the retrieve to be a basic exercise, I will treat it as one for more advanced work and discuss it at a later stage.

The preciseness of heelwork is something that is determined by the owner. Although domestic loose lead walking may be sufficient to satisfy many owners, the principals with competitive heelwork are the same. It is just the degree of accuracy that changes, and therefore the amount of work to be put in.

A competitive recall may differ considerably from that of the domestic 'come back when called', but some of the elements are identical with the domestic requirement having to allow for greater distractions to give specially constructed elements for practical daily events.

To some owners any one of the stay exercises may be felt as unnecessary for their purposes; but it could be unwise to leave any of them out of the equation.

Table (a) (overleaf) illustrates the complete breakdown of the basic exercises into their elements where it will be seen that certain elements are common to more than one exercise. This can help with the planning of a training programme. It will also be seen that each element is considered to be *active* or *static* and in some cases the element can be divided into two sub elements where one is *active* and the other is *static*. What classifies the *active* and *static* elements or sub-elements?

An *active* element is one that requires the correct movement from the dog in response to the owner's instruction. These *active* movements usually require a certain amount of excited inducement from the owner to achieve a changed canine response. The amount of excited inducement from the owner will depend on the dog and the commitment to his partner and the prevailing conditions; also the level of training and the nature or strength of any distractions.

A *static* element is one where the owner requests no canine movement although the level of attention between dog and owner should in most situations be at the highest level. The instruction may well be to 'stay' (static) until an *active* element has been introduced. This may be for a lengthy period,

BASIC EXERCISES
ELEMENTS FOR EACH EXERCISE – Table (a)

ELEMENTS	HEEL WORK	RECALL	SIT STAY	DOWN STAY	STAND STAY
Generate attention to the owner	Static and waiting instruction	Static and waiting instruction	Static and waiting instruction	Static and waiting instruction	Static and waiting instruction
Dog stands as and where instructed					Active – Static or remains Static
Dog moves from the sit and walk at heel with owner	Active				
Dog executes turns-left, right, about at owner's side	Active				
Dog sits on halt at owner's left side	Active – Static				
Dog stays while owner leaves dog		Static	Static	Static	Static
Dog to await recall from owner		Static			
Dog returns to owner		Active			
Dog sits in front of owner		Active–Static			
Dog goes round to heel and sits at owner's left side		Active–Static			
Dog stays in position on return of owner			Static	Static	Static
Dog responds to **FINISH**	Active	Active	Active	Active	Active

Note: Some elements are linked or subdivided with Static and Active components.
In themselves, these components require change of approach by the owner.

as in each of the Stay exercises, although there can often be the case when an *active* element (or sub-element) will immediate follow a *static* one. With a *static* element, the owner's attitude is one of a quiet and settled, but purposeful, appearance creating a situation where it will induce calmness and a 'stress free' feeling within the dog.

The immediate change of attitude from the owner between *active* and *static* must be fully appreciated and applied with the appropriate feeling behind it, if it is to be fully effective. *This point cannot be put too strongly as it is at the centre of canine understanding.*

We can take the exercise of heelwork as an example, and break it down into the relevant elements and sub-elements to assess the actual requirements.

Note: Any of the basic exercises, with the exception of Generating Attention, will normally start with the dog on the lead beside the owner.

The elements that make up the Heelwork routine can also be referred to in Table [a].

1. GENERATING THE DOG'S ATTENTION

We are asking the dog to be prepared to start the exercise and, at that precise moment, we are not asking for any movement from him. This is therefore a *static* element while he is waiting for further instructions. There will be a measure of anticipation in the owner's voice to induce the feeling and watchfulness from the dog that indicates, 'I am ready and waiting, what's next?'

2. DOG TO SIT AT OWNER'S LEFT SIDE

This is an *active* sub-element by having or putting the dog into the sit position. While in that position it now becomes a *static* sub-element and waiting for the Heelwork to begin.

The *active* sub-element requires the excited inducement to achieve a charged canine response and the *static* sub-element requires a situation where it will induce calmness and a stress free feeling within the dog; but with a strong sense of responsibility.

3. DOG MOVES FROM THE SIT AND WALKS TO HEEL

Rising from the sit position into walking to heel with the owner is now an *active* element with all the body and verbal encouragement that may be required to achieve this element.

4. DOG, WITH OWNER, EXECUTES RIGHT, LEFT AND ABOUT TURNS

Being an *active* element and with the dog maintaining this position at the owner's side is a continuation of the previous element. Both parties require concentration and the owner's body movements, along with verbal encouragement, also encouragement for the dog to execute the various turns.

5. DOG SITS ON HALT AT THE OWNER'S LEFT SIDE

This could be an intermediate 'stop' during the training routine or it can be in preparation for completion of the exercise. Like element No.2 this carries both an *active* and a *static* sub-element. The dog is induced into an immediate 'sit' (*active*) then followed by a controlled and restrained period (*static*) in preparation for the release on completion of the exercise. Again the change in attitude from the owner is very important to create a proper interpretation of requirements from the dog. An excited movement 'sit' and then controlled composure to await further instructions.

6. DOG'S RESPONSE TO THE FINISH OF THE EXERCISE

This can be a highly *active* element where both dog and owner complete the exercise with a show of great pleasure at the fulfillment of a satisfactory conclusion.

UTILISING AND TRAINING ELEMENTS

An examination of the Table (a) for the breakdown of the basic exercises will highlight the elements that are common to more than one exercise. The training of an element for one exercise can accomplish the requirements of another. The best example is that of 'Generating Attention On The Owner'. It is true that with any exercise or element of an exercise we must be able to generate the dog's attention; without that, we can achieve nothing of any significance. It is therefore essential to appreciate that this element is *the most important factor* in dog training or behaviour management.

The number of elements that are common to two particular exercises will be seen by the tie up between the recall and the sit stay. In some cases an element can be trained in a manner that covers both exercises, but with other elements, it may be better to concentrate on one before considering the application within the other exercise.

An example where I have seen an exercise ruined for the lives of some dogs is the Sit and Stay.

It is quite natural to train various basic exercises through their elementary stages during the same training session. Not only is it natural, but also it is convenient during a half hour session to include recall and stay exercises.

The problem arises when the dog is left at the sit while the owner walks away in preparation for recalling the dog. At the same stage of training the dog is expected to sit and stay for a period while the owner creates distance between himself and his dog before returning to him.

With the methods in use by quite a few owners (at the direction of their instructors), the recall exercise starts with the dog being left at the sit before the recall takes place. I have often heard it said that if the owner uses the verbal expression of 'sit and wait' for the recall and 'sit and stay' for the sit/stay exercise, the dogs will understand the difference. This is a sensible approach, but too much is expected of it too early for many dogs.

However, if we train the recall with the dog being free to move, on or off the lead or long line, the full exercise can be trained to a very high standard with the exception of having the dog sit and wait to be recalled. At the same time the sit/stay exercise can be trained in a conventional way.

Until a good, solid sit/stay has been achieved the dog should *never* be recalled from an instructed stay position.

When both exercises have been perfected without the 'sit and wait' for the recall the dog can then be trained to utilise the stay with the 'break' being brought into by means of a particular method which will not damage the sit/stay exercise. This will be more fully explained within the appropriate training procedure.

Chapter 12

DEVELOPING TRAINING ROUTINES

gain, we start with the basic training exercises and initially it would be realistic to take each of these exercises and understand their objectives. The basic exercises and their objectives are now listed:

1. Generating attention
2. Recall (come back when called)
3. Elementary heelwork (Loose lead walking)
4. Sit and stay
5. Down and stay
6. Stay standing

Each exercise has an objective and it will be noted that although the titles on which the exercises are based, control requirements and the depth of training (precision) can be varied to suit the purpose of the owners. The expertise for Obedience competition work differs from that of other forms of competition, just as professional requirements for police or security can differ. Although training of the family pet can be much less regimented, there is still a distinct requirement for an immediate and purposeful canine response to each situation.

Exercise 1: Generating attention

OBJECTIVE

To ensure that the dog will give the owner his full attention when it is required and will respond to any follow up activity. To give the dog some purpose for giving his attention to the owner and, as a follow up activity, the dog must be prepared to watch and follow the owner's every movement. During this procedure the owner's movement will develop so that he will be alternating between walking backwards then forwards. In the early stages there will be much more backwards movement than forwards. This approach is also an important introduction to both the recall and heelwork exercises, but it also includes an introduction to the stay exercises.

Exercise 2: Recall

OBJECTIVE

To ensure that the dog will give his full attention to the owner when required and the dog will respond to the call to go back to him.

Exercise 3: Heelwork (On lead)

OBJECTIVE

The dog to walk reasonably close and level with the owner at his left side. This should be carried out on a loose lead with the level of attention that has the dog aware of, and reacts to, any changes of the owner's walking directions. The dog should also be prepared to sit at the owner's left side as and when required.

Exercise 4: Sit and stay

OBJECTIVE

To ensure that the dog will go into the sit position when required and stay sitting, without changing position or moving, until he has been released

Exercise 5: Down and stay

OBJECTIVE

To ensure that the dog will go into the down position when required and to stay down, without changing position or moving, until he has been released.

Exercise 6: Stay standing

OBJECTIVE

To ensure that the dog will remain in a standing position without moving in any direction, even during moments of stress. Also remaining until the owner considers that the situation no longer demands this form of restraint.

Note: The training of the stay exercise is there for various reasons and owners may wish to develop any one to a higher degree than the others.

To leave a dog sitting is part of the programme of training to help ensure stability and control. To have a dog sit for a short spell can be very convenient for many purposes.

To have a dog going down and staying is the most comfortable position for leaving a dog for a short period of time. A dog is normally much more comfortable when left at the down rather than in the sit position.

To have a dog standing when requested has a number of advantages, quite apart from showing in the breed ring. To stand for examination or grooming is a benefit worth working for; however, the training to have a dog stay where he is when out on the loose for pleasure or exercise, is an extremely useful feature. Under stressful situations, it may be necessary to command the dog to stay where he is because of the dangers due to bicycles, a child or other dogs in the area. Within any of the stay exercises, the stationary element is crucial to success. It is demanding on the dog and requires a very balanced outlook from the owner.

These are the final objectives for a basic training course, but within these objectives there are progressive stages to be worked and assessed. These progressive stages may be considered as objectives on their own account, but to avoid confusion they will be called targets. The time taken over each stage of training, or to reach each of the targets varies considerably from dog to dog, or from owner to owner. When handled within the context of a training class there is usually one week of training between the achievements of each target. However, the time spent for each stage is dependent on the time available for training and the progress being made. The training routines for the basic exercises will now be given.

Master training schedule

As instructors, we all have our own ideas about when to introduce specific elements from the basic exercises into the training schedule. Although some instructors in the past did not seem to have a plan to operate their schedule and, as a result, they created conflicting situations that caused more problems than they solved, I think that most are now applying a more enlightened approach.

There are a few different ways of presenting the approach that I apply, and I select the approach that suits the occasion.

My schedule (programme) works on an eight session series of tuition opportunities with each session bringing in the appropriate targets for the exercises involved. This is shown in the 'Programme of Training Sessions' opposite'.

Within this book, it is felt to be more appropriate to concentrate on each exercise as a single entity. However, each stage of every basic exercise is correctly identified with its introduction and progress throughout an eight-session programme. The Master Training Schedule is as follows:

The Programme of Training Sessions – Table (b)

	STAGE ONE	STAGE TWO	STAGE THREE	STAGE FOUR	STAGE FIVE	STAGE SIX	STAGE SEVEN	STAGE EIGHT
1. GENERATING ATTENTION	1(a)	1(b)	1(c)	1(d)	1(e)	1(f)	1(g)	1(h)
2. RECALL			2(a)	2(a)	2(b)	2(c)	2(d)	2(d)
3. HEELWORK					3(a)	3(b)	3(c)	3(d)
4. SIT AND STAY	4(a)	4(b)	4(c)	4(d)	4(e)	4(f)	4(g)	4(g)
5. DOWN AND STAY		5(a)	5(b)	5(c)	5(d)	5(e)	5(f)	5(g)
6. STAY STANDING					6(a)	6(a)	6(b)	6(b)

These training exercises are detailed in the following chapter, pages 92 to 139.

It will be seen from the schedule that exercises are introduced to coincide with the stage development of the Generating Attention exercise and taking it into the fifth session before the training of all the exercises takes place.

Quite apart from the logic of such a progression this method creates a gradual introduction for the dog and ensures that he is not expected to learn too much at the earliest stages of the learning process. It may be appropriate to consider as a guide, that each stage takes a week to learn and consolidate before moving to the next.

Chapter 13

TRAINING

The following training routines are intended to cover the basic exercises as discussed in the previous chapter, and it is important to recognise that the training stages include a number, from 1 to 6 for each of the exercises and the letters in brackets (a) to (h) to indicate the actual stage in training. Generating Attention from 1 (a) to 1 (h) and the Recall going from 2 (a) to 2 (d) and so on.

Although the training described for the basic objectives does not take the owner through to a competition level of training the approach gives a solid foundation for each of the six exercises as applied where the owner's particular requirements are much more demanding.

Note: Throughout all stages of this training programme it is strongly advised that owners work within the sequence and timing of the Master Training Schedule in Chapter 12

SECTION 1

GENERATING ATTENTION

Starting at stage one from the Master Training Schedule (page 91)

EQUIPMENT – Training Element 1 (a)

- Collar
- Lead
- Toys/titbits (if required)

TARGET

At the end of this stage, the dog will be able to start on the lead from any relaxed position (standing, sitting, lying down or just moseying around). The dog should respond attentively to the call of his name and move on a loose lead towards his owner as he is moving backwards. The owner should be giving full encouragement as the dog is moving towards him. If possible, this operation should be carried out with minor or no distractions to the dog and for periods of five to ten seconds.

Notes:

(a) Backward movement does not need to be in a straight line, although at this stage, about, precise left or right turns should not be a requirement.

(b) The training of this exercise is to be the basis of control at any and all times. Major distractions are unlikely to take place at this stage and it is also advisable that the owner does not become reliant on food or toys. It is important to achieve total owner commitment at this early stage, the use of food and toys is likely to dilute that commitment. Toys or food can however be used as a reward if desired when applied along with praise immediately on completion of the individual training activity.

PRINCIPAL ACTIVITY

With the dog on the lead, the action to be applied is that of the owner making a smart movement backwards. The dog's name should become the principal attention generator, but initially, it may also be necessary to apply the following action:

- To be accompanied by a tap on the dog's hindquarters.
- Or a short, sharp jerk on the lead. This may be considered by many to be an outdated procedure, but it is still valid when advisable and, when correctly carried out at this stage along with enthusiastic praise.

A continuation of this backward movement to be carried out for a few seconds in a manner that ensures the dog's attention is maintained. If canine attention has been allowed to deviate from the owner due to some unexpected distraction, a change of direction to left or right and away from the distraction will probably be necessary along with any of the usual verbal, visual or/and physical activities from a highly committed owner to regenerate full attention.

Although intended distractions should not be included at this stage, it can be difficult on occasions to train without any that are likely to affect a dog's attention.

Distractions will always be present at group training sessions and even out in the open, a tussock of grass will harbour smells that can be attractive to a dog that is not fully committed. However, boredom in itself, can be turned to advantage for this training routine.

WORKING TECHNIQUES

The use and timing of the dog's name is of the utmost importance. The use of the dog's name *must* be developed as the principal means of gaining the dog's attention. The name should be used with urgency, but not with harshness. Although great volume is not required, there should be sufficient penetration and urgency to be effective.

The use of the name is applied *immediately* prior to the backward movement and, if it is required, a tap on the dog's hindquarters or a jerk on the lead. There should be no time lag between the call of the name and the physical application of movement. The dog's attention is maintained at this stage by the almost continual use of the voice with encouraging phrases to have him follow his fully committed owner. A phrase such as, 'come on son, *hurry up*', and repeated or changed as necessary can be used. Suitable facial expressions and physical movements should accompany this vocal inducement. The vocal communication with a dog is most important. In this case, the 'come on son,' is with great urgency, possibly demanding, but not threatening. The follow through with, '*hurry up*', is a counter, and is applied in much more pleasant and encouraging manner. Voice and the variations in deflection, are always part of the principal means of communication with a dog.

HANDLING TECHNIQUES

The handling of the lead along with hand and arm actions, also body posture, are equally important features for generating and maintaining canine attention.

The loop at the end of the lead should be over the thumb of the right hand and, held when necessary, in the clenched fist. When the owner's backward movement is taking place, the dog is expected to follow attentively and with enthusiasm. If practical, the hands and lead should be kept low with the lead/collar attachment below the dog's lower jaw. With the palms of the hands facing upwards, the owner should be using encouraging movements with fingers and arms. The hands should be in a position that will be easily attracted to the dog's eyes.

The dog is encouraged to move faster than the owner, so that he will finish close to him with them facing each other. In achieving this situation the lead must be kept loose, but gradually taken in by both left and right hands in a manner which will allow the owner to drop the lead, except for the loop on the right thumb, when alternative action is required. This alternative action can be utilised to counter canine distraction during backward movement. Progress from one stage to another should only be made when the previous stage has been achieved to the individual's satisfaction. *Success always deserves appreciation.*

Activity Illustrating loop over thumb.

Principal observations

* Holding the lead in this position helps to create open-handed approach when required.

Activity Showing success in generating and maintaining the dog's attention

Principal observations

- With the palms of the hands facing upwards, the owner, along with her voice, is using encouraging movements with body, fingers and arms.

- Continued response from the dog

- Position of loop over right thumb, which enables the hand to be clenched and opened at will.

Stage Two (Generating Attention) – Training Element 1 (b)

(Planning for strong distractions)

EQUIPMENT

- Collar
- Lead
- Toys/titbits (if required)

TARGET

At the end of this stage, the dog should be able to respond, despite strong distractions, to the call of his name and move on a loose lead as the owner is moving backwards and drawing the dog to him. The dog's attention should be held during this operation and for five to ten seconds at a time.

PRINCIPAL ACTIVITY

The activity is a repeat of Target 1 (a) but with the application of some stronger distractions. These distractions can be applied within a training group or on a one to one basis.

A member of the family or the presence of another dog can be utilised as a strong distraction. The attraction between the two dogs can be friendly or aggressively based to suit the circumstances.

The owner, with the dog on the lead, can start from some ten to fifteen paces from the distraction and walk directly towards it. Handling Techniques described in target 1 (a) must be used immediately to counter any attempt by the dog to move ahead of the owner or to pull on the lead. With distractions, firm handling may be required along with immediate praise when the dog co-operates with enthusiasm. Remember that canine enthusiasm can be a reaction to the correct form of human enthusiasm and commitment.

HANDLING TECHNIQUES

In addition to the details given in 1 (a) and already practised, alternatives to the jerk on the lead can be:

1. To give a positive, but not a harsh slap with the flat of the hand on the hindquarters as his name is being called to gain the dog's attention. This to be followed immediately by backwards movement and encouragement to follow as required.

2. In the most extreme cases and where other means have failed, it is important that success be achieved and the following alternative is therefore suggested. While the dog is on the lead, smartly grip the loose skin at the groin in the hand and squeeze sharply for a *split second* and simultaneously call the dog's name and, at the same time, move backwards quickly with encouragement to follow.

Note: The loose skin at the groin is normally a very tender area and will result in an immediate reaction. However, a dog with a sharp aggressive nature may turn to bite the perpetrator and this approach may not be advisable where this type of nature has not been properly controlled. It is very important that the party controlling the dog during this activity has sufficient experience to handle such a situation with confidence.

Activity Owner moving forward to tap dog's hindquarters.

Principal observations

- Speedy but quiet movement to take dog by surprise.

- Owner moving back and encouraging the dog to follow.

- The immediate response from the dog.

Activity The nip in the groin to achieve the effect on a dog that could be less responsive.

Principal observations

- Response expected to be as illustrated.

- A dog with a sharp aggressive nature may turn to and this approach may *not* be advisable unless any aggressiveness is under control.

Stage Three (Generating Attention) – Training Element 1 (c)

EQUIPMENT

- Collar
- Lead
- Toys/titbits (if required)

TARGET

At the end of this stage the dog will be able to change direction with the owner. After moving backwards with the dog following on the lead a change to forward movement should result in the dog turning to fall in at the owner's left side for a few paces.

Use alternating owner movements of backwards then forwards with varying distractions for a period of up to 30 seconds.

PRINCIPAL ACTIVITY

This stage brings in the first step of heelwork training or loose lead walking. However, forward movement after moving away from a distraction gives the dog the opportunity to reactivate his interest in the distraction. Any return of this interest must be controlled by another change to backward movement.

When alternating between backward and forward movements the backward movement should take in at least six paces but many more may be required to ensure that attention is maintained. Forward movement is controlled by the dog's ability to maintain an attentive position with his head approximately in line with the owner's left leg.

During this activity, half a minute of full attention should be attainable without the dog's attention wandering away from his owner at any time.

HANDLING TECHNIQUES

When changing from backward to forward movement, the owner should move to the right (dog's left side) so that the dog can turn towards his owner's left side as they are passing each other. The left arm can move out to the side so that the left hand is of assistance in guiding the dog into place.

As soon as both dog and owner are moving forward in the same direction the pattern of lead control is again important. With the loop still over the right thumb it can be gathered in the right hand so that the surplus is at the owner's right side and does not become a hindrance.

With both arms extended downwards and relaxed, the hands should be in front of each leg. At this early stage in training there should be approximately six to eight inches of lead between the left and right hands and a minimum of lead between the dog's collar and the left hand. However, the lead between dog and owner should not be tight. The left hand can hold the lead, be used as a guide for the lead or taken off the lead and be freely used for encouragement as and how the circumstances demand.

On occasions, forward movement can be interrupted by a halt every single step or every double steps. The dog is not being initially asked to sit during these punctuated stops, but should take these steps with the owner and stay still, standing or sitting at the dog's pleasure, with every momentary stop. Any failure to do so will require a smart backward movement and this should be continued until he reacts correctly to the owner's movements. Distance from a distraction has a great deal of effect. The closer the dog is to the distraction the greater is the need to have the dog concentrate and remain attentively.

Full activity: This group makes up a sequence of movements for a single function of owner drawing the dog as she moves backwards [pic A opposite], then enticing the dog to her left as she changes from backward to forward movement [pic B]. The dog swings round [pic C] and completes the movement by coming into 'heel' at her left side [pic D].

**Principal observations
throughout the series**

- Position of loop over right thumb.
- Application of hands to draw dog while giving visual and verbal encouragement.
- Throughout the procedure, the owner's left hand should be positioned so that it can be the object of the dog's attention.
- The owner applies a watchful eye on the dog's reactions.

Stage Four (Generating Attention) – Training Element 1 (d)

EQUIPMENT

- Collar
- Lead
- Toys/titbits (if required)

TARGET

At the end of this stage, the dog will be able to sit smartly at the owner's left side when he halts on completion of a forward movement.

PRINCIPAL ACTIVITY

The previous target being accomplished with enthusiasm and satisfaction now leads on to a controlled finish, that of having the dog sit nicely at the owner's left side when he halts.

The details for achieving this sit should be accomplished quite independently of this routine under training exercise sit and stay at the level of target 4 (c).

It may initially be necessary for the owner to give physical assistance along with the instruction to sit and ensure that the dog immediately responds when the owner halts.

HANDLING TECHNIQUE

This is best performed by using the following approach. Within a step of halting, the owner to move his right hand over to hold the lead as close to the collar as is practical. This controls the movement of the dog's forequarters as the owner halts and releases the left hand to push in at the left side of the dog's croup to ensure a quick and controlled sit. The timing of a verbal instruction to sit, at the second of stopping, will soon ensure that the dog will respond without physical assistance.

As soon as the dog sits, gentle praise should be applied while the dog is made to hold the sit position for some five seconds. Abundant praise can then be given as soon as the dog is released from the finished position.

Activity Putting the dog into the sitting position. Within a step of halting, the owner to move his right hand over to hold the lead as close to the collar as is practical. This controls the movement of the dog's forequarters as the owner halts, also releases the left hand to push in at the left side of the dog's croup to ensure a quick and controlled sit.

Principal observations

- Right hand controls head at the collar.

- Left hand at the groin applies pressure to ensure a prompt sit
- With a small dog the owner would have to get down to its level.

Activity Lead handling when dog is in the sit position.

Principal observations

- Distance between hands with arms approximately in front of legs.
- Excess lead at right side.
- Minimum lead between left hand and dog.

Stage Five (Generating Attention) – Training Element 1 (e)

EQUIPMENT

- Collar
- Lead
- Toys/titbits (if required)

TARGET

At the end of this stage, on the verbal instruction, the dog will be able to sit in front of the owner and facing him as the owner halts on completion of a backwards movement. Dog to be reasonably close to the owner's body after an attentive backward movement.

PRINCIPAL ACTIVITY AND HANDLING TECHNIQUE

As the dog has already been training to sit at the owner's left side and to do so without physical assistance, there should not be any difficulty in getting him to sit in front. Although physical handling can be applied to achieve the objective, inducements should achieve a much more attentive frame of mind.

Initially, while on the lead, the dog will be sitting at the owner's left side. The owner should then move round so that he is standing close and in front of the dog. The owner can gain the dog's attention with a titbit; a toy should only be used on completion of that part of the training session and when direct control is no longer required. Owner should then inch backwards about half to one step and draw the dog back with him using verbal and visual encouragement along with a titbit or some other form of inducement.

The dog will not have a real chance to stand up with this short movement forward to maintain closeness to the owner. The verbal instruction to sit and the visual aid with the inducement to draw the dog's head up should achieve the close sit position. Reward to be as before.

When the short movement becomes easily accomplished, the owner to move backwards a few paces with the dog following attentively, then to halt and encourage the dog to sit close to and facing the owner. This procedure can then be developed into the full attention generating routine.

Stage Six (Generating Attention) – Training Element 1 (f)

EQUIPMENT

- Collar
- Short or long trailing line
- Toys/titbits (if required)

TARGET

At the end of this stage the dog will be able to respond attentively with a 6ft line (or long line if preferred) attached to his collar instead of the lead. The use of minor distractions can be considered as confidence is gained.

With the loose end of the line dragging on the ground the dog should respond to the call of his name and also to the owner's backward movements. Sits should be avoided for a while and the routine similar to the Element 1 (a) would be suitable. The dog's attention should be held for about ten seconds before completion.

PRINCIPAL ACTIVITY AND HANDLING TECHNIQUE

This target is principally a method of assessing the control that has been achieved through this routine. It is also a means of gaining confidence in the owner's ability to control the dog without the back up of a lead.

The target to be practised initially by holding the end of the line as the owner would with a lead and, when a fluent response is achieved, the line can be dropped for the remainder of the training period of this routine. The end of the line can be picked and dropped at any time the performance is deemed to be unsatisfactory. If a long line is preferred, and if advisable, a piece of wood can be attached at any suitable length from the dog to create that sense of responsibility.

This target should then be practised successfully for sessions covering four or five days without holding the line before considering the performance to be satisfactory.

Activity Dog with a short trailing line.

Principal observations

- The line can be allowed to drag or can be picked up at any time to apply physical control if and when necessary.

Activity Getting the dog into the sitting position after backward movement.

Principal observations

- Hands together central and close to the body to help achieve a central and straight sit. Can also be applied with titbit being drawn up at the height of the dog's nose.

Stage Seven (Generating Attention) – Training Element 1 (g)

EQUIPMENT

- Collar
- Short or long trailing line
- Toys/titbits (if required)

TARGET

At the end of this stage the dog will he able to respond attentively with short line attached to his collar instead of the lead and by utilising stronger distractions.

With the loose end of the line dragging on the ground the dog should respond to backward and forward movements and also to sit at the owner's left side at the halt on completion of the owner's forward movement and, on completion of backward movement, to sit in front of the owner at the halt.

PRINCIPAL ACTIVITY AND HANDLING TECHNIQUES

This target is a continuation of the previous training and should initially be practised while holding the line, particularly to achieve attentive sits on each halt. When a fluent response is achieved the line can be dropped for the remainder of the routine period. Any deterioration in response will require a return to holding of the line.

This target should be practised successfully for four or five daily sessions without holding the line to ensure consolidation of the response. The end of the line can however, be picked and dropped when the performance is deemed to be unsatisfactory.

Stage Eight (Generating Attention) – Training Element 1 (h)

EQUIPMENT

- Collar
- Short trailing line, activity cord or loop
- Toys/titbits (if required)

TARGET

At the end of this stage, without any attachment to the collar, the dog will be able to respond to backward and forward movements with the appropriate sits at the halts on completion of either of these backward and forward movements.

PRINCIPAL ACTIVITY AND HANDLING TECHNIQUES

This activity along with the handling technique can be a repeat of the previous stage, but instead of a cord attached to the collar, initially the short trailing line, activity loop or the activity cord, which can be *laced through the collar ring* and utilised as a lead to start the process. After a few seconds of a fluent response the clip end of the line remains kept in the hand while the other end is released. Collect the line from the clip end (or cord from the loop) to have the dog free so that the remainder of the routine can be continued as per Stage 1 (g) without any physical connecting link between dog and owner.

Again greater encouragement with voice and body actions may be required to ensure that none of the previous performances are lost.

Activity Use of activity cord.

Principal observations

- Loop of cord in right thumb.
- Ability to drop the free end when required.

Activity Use of activity loop attached to the collar.

Principal observations

- Loop of cord in held in the left hand.
- Ability to drop the loop when required.

Section 2

BASIC RECALL (or Come Back When Called)

Starting at stages three and four from the Master Training Schedule (Page 91).

Note: Much of the basic work has been carried out during the training for Attention Generating and it is important that this foundation is recognised before starting this routine.

EQUIPMENT – Training Element 2 (a)

- Collar
- Lead
- Long and short trailing lines (weight attachment optional)
- Flexi-lead
- Toys/titbits (if required)

TARGET

At the end of this stage, while attached to a Flexi-lead or long line, the dog will be able to respond to the call of his name and the instruction to 'come', and also to return with enthusiasm while various distractions come into play. In the early stages of training, a flexi-lead or a long line can be used to suit the requirements of the dog and owner.

PRINCIPAL ACTIVITY AND HANDLING TECHNIQUE

With the flexi-lead attached to the collar, the dog should be given freedom to move away and show interest in some distraction somewhere within the full length of the line. Before the end of the line has been reached the stop button to be pressed by the owner as he calls his dog. He immediately moves backwards as he releases the stop button, and applies the attention generating routine. The flexi-lead line will automatically retract and prevent the loose line from catching in the dog's legs.

When the dog is responding immediately without the need to press the flexi button, a long (30ft) line can be used to replace the flexi-lead. This is attached to the dog's collar and on occasions, is allowed to drag along the ground. This can create greater working distances between dog and owner.

As the line is being allowed to drag along the ground an excitable dog can still cause situations that are difficult to control. In such cases a piece of wood can be tied on the free end to create tension when dragged along by the dog. This in itself will often produce a more responsible attitude from the dog. The larger the piece of wood the greater the tension on the line and a greater sense of responsibility. There are situations when a short trailing line with a piece of wood on the end may be an advantage.

When the dog is showing interest in some distraction, the owner can pick up the line at some suitable distance from the dog and, with purpose, call his name, if necessary he can also give a sharp tug on the line (similar to the actions with a lead during the attention generating routine) at the same time moving backwards with highly encouraging overtures so that the dog is induced to follow. The owner should use everything he has, verbal and visual, to induce an immediate and willing response.

The line should never be kept tight unless it is to prevent the dog from moving away, and the dog should never be pulled in at any stage. The line should be kept as low as is practical and again be utilised in the same manner as the lead during the attention generating routine. As the dog comes in at a greater pace than the owner's speed when moving backwards, the extra line can be passed through the owner's hands to ensure that he maintains control if the dog changes his mind and stops or attempts to move away. Great pleasure must be shown when the dog is coming back and when he finishes beside the owner. Praise and other rewards will show the appreciation for success.

This approach can be applied, until it is certain that the dog will return from all forms and degrees of distraction. When this has been achieved the dog should then be called back under various conditions without the need to have a piece of wood on the end or to pick up the line.

Activity Controlled fun and being recalled on the flexi-lead.

Principal observation

The line seems to be taut because of the rewind mechanism on the flexi. The dog is not, and should never be physically pulled in.

Activity Application of flexi-lead

Principal observation

- Thumb on stop button to control the dog's forward movement.

Activity Nearing completion of the recall on the flexi-lead.

Principal observation

Visual and vocal encouragement has helped to bring the dog in so that the throw toy can be taken by the owner.

Activity Application of the trailing long line can be used in many situations and the attachment of a suitable article on the end can help to achieve a sense of responsibility within the dog.

Principal observation

Care must be taken with an unruly dog to ensure that the line does not danger the owner or other walkers, although getting wrapped round the dog's own legs will help him to realise that he can be causing his own problems.

Stage Five (Recall) – Training Element 2 (b)

EQUIPMENT
- Collar
- Lead
- Long trailing line
- Flexi-lead if desired
- Toys/titbits (if required)

TARGET

At the end of this stage, while the dog is attached to a trailing long line, which can be free and dragging on the ground, the owner to move backwards a few paces at a time. The dog will be able to follow the owner as he is given encouragement. Titbits can be used every few steps. Dog to maintain full attention during movement and with each halt. Various distractions can be applied as the dog responds to the procedure.

PRINCIPAL ACTIVITY AND HANDLING TECHNIQUE

During the early stages it may be necessary to return to the lead for the back-ward movement as it is applied with the attention generating routine. Praise and the option of titbits spaced at every few paces along with encouragement both verbal and physical can be applied to maintain the dog's attention.

The dog may stand or sit as he wishes. The objective at this stage is to maintain the dog's attention.

When this has been successfully achieved the owner should give longer periods of backward movement but continue to maintain the dog's attention for a full five seconds every time he stops. Any deviation of the dog's attention, due to distractions or not, must immediately be countered by a change of movement away from the cause of the distraction with the owner doing everything he can to regain or maintain that attention. Always reward with praise – with or without titbits.

If the lead has been used and the dog is responding consistently and with satisfaction the owner can continue by carrying out a similar sequence of activity with the long line to attain success at greater distances from the dog before calling him in.

Stage Six (Recall) – Training Element 2 (c)

EQUIPMENT

- Collar
- Lead
- Short trailing line
- Toys/titbits (if required)

TARGET

At the end of this stage with a 6ft line attached to his collar, the dog will be able to respond to the call of his name and also come back when called from varying distances and stay beside the owner on his return. Minor distractions may be applied.

PRINCIPAL ACTIVITY AND HANDLING TECHNIQUE

The importance of a successful and consolidated situation with the previous target 2 (b) will now become apparent and, as with any other stage of training, the owner must he prepared to go back to previous targets if problems become evident.

Use of the short line attached to the collar is the connecting link between the use of the long line and complete freedom.

Apply the same principles as utilised in target 2 (a) and 2 (b) but maintain shorter distances between dog and owner, always avoid situations where a refusal can be expected. Build up on distance and with distractions that are within the capabilities of the dog and owner's progress in training.

Situations with failure to come back will require the application of target 6 (b) to stay standing as an alternative to a recall.

As the dogs respond to their satisfaction, some owners find it useful to gradually cut pieces off the length of line. As confidence grows it can be shortened with only about ten inches left. This gives the dog the feeling that the line is still a controlling factor.

Activity Returning on the short trailing line.

Principal observation

This particular dog feels the restraint of the line and he returns in a subdued but controlled manner. Other dogs may require a dragging attachment to the line to obtain a suitable frame of mind.

Stages Seven and Eight (Recall) – Training Element 2 (d)

EQUIPMENT

- Collar
- Lead
- Toys/titbits (if required)

TARGET

At the end of this stage, while the dog is completely free, he will be able to respond to the call of his name and also to come back when called from varying distances and stay beside the owner on his return. Minor to major distractions may be applied.

PRINCIPAL ACTIVITY AND HANDLING TECHNIQUE

The recall from a completely free situation is just a continuation of the previous target 2 (c) with the use of increasing distances between dog and owner, also variations in the magnitude of the distraction.

It must be remembered that success builds up confidence in the owner and control over his dog; but over confidence has its own dangers. If this results in a failure, the owner will require to go back to the 6ft cord or even the long line situation if necessary to rebuild control and confidence. The owner does not need to remain stationary while the dog is coming in and he can move backwards to help induce an enthusiastic response.

As target 1 (e) (Stage (5) of attention generating) has already been accomplished, the use of titbits or a suitable toy will soon establish an attentive sit in front with sufficient time for praise before completing the exercise and attaching the lead.

Activity Dog being called by the owner while completely free.

Principal observation

- Owner's hand and body actions along with verbal inducement ensures that the dog responds with enthusiasm.

Activity Owner moves backwards and continues to draw the dog.

Principal observation

- The owner's backward movement with verbal and continued visual inducements ensures that the the dog's enthusiasm and response is maintained.

Section 3

HEELWORK (Loose Lead Walking)

Starting at stage five from the Master Training Schedule (page 91)

Note: Throughout this training programme it is strongly advised that you work within the sequence and timing of the Master Training Schedule.

Stage Five (Heelwork) Training Element 3 (a)

EQUIPMENT

- Collar
- Lead
- Toys/titbits (if required)

(Accomplish Element 1 (c) before commencement of this routine)

TARGET

At the end of this stage, while on the lead, the dog will be able to walk reasonably close to the owner's left side and on a loose lead for a spell of some fifteen to twenty seconds without the need of changing to the attention generating backward movement. Owner movement should be in a straight line or a large left hand circle.

PRINCIPAL ACTIVITY AND HANDLING TECHNIQUE

The principal activity and handling technique of target 1 (c) of the attention generating routine, is the foundation on which the target is built. During any forward and backward movement the owner must concentrate on the dog's response to try and prevent deviation of attention, or to catch such deviation if a distraction overtakes the situation. At this stage it is advisable to start from a situation where the dog has freedom on the lead. The activity should be applied and developed so that, after the initial start, backward movement need only be utilised when there is an indication from the dog that he is going to lose some of that attention.

Continuous owner concentration should be limited to spells of no greater than thirty seconds without a reasonable break.

Satisfaction is attained when the dog can complete some fifteen to twenty seconds without losing his attention resulting in the need to apply lead control or backward movement.

Activity Calling and guiding dog in to heel.

Principal observation

The use of the owner's left hand to guide the dog and verbally encourage in to heel.

Stage Six (Heelwork) – Training Element 3 (b)

EQUIPMENT

- Collar
- Lead
- Toys/titbits (if required)

TARGET

At the end of this stage the dog will be able to carry out attentive loose lead walking for a period of at least thirty seconds. To finish by sitting at the owner's left side when he halts.

PRINCIPAL ACTIVITY AND HANDLING TECHNIQUE

(Accomplish Element 4 (a) before commencement of this routine)

As target 1 (d) from the attention generating routine has already been achieved, the dog is able to sit at the owner's left side as instructed when the owner halts. However, at this stage, to maintain the dog's enthusiasm, it is advisable not to start from the sit position, but to start where the dog has relative freedom on the end of the lead.

Within a step of coming to a halt the owner moves his right hand over to hold the lead very close to the collar. This controls the movement of the dog's forequarters as the owner halts and releases the left hand to push at the left side of the dog's croup to ensure a quick and controlled sit (already described in 1 (d)).

The correct timing of a verbal instruction will soon ensure that the dog will respond without physical assistance. Gentle praise should be applied while the dog is made to remain in the sit position for five seconds. Gentle praise can be given when the dog is released from the finished sit position.

A continuation of this activity should result in longer spells of forward movement before stopping and applying the canine SIT position until the dog will sit automatically when instructed to halt.

Activity Putting the dog into the sitting position. (See element 1 (d) for fuller details and principal observations).

Activity Sitting at the halt when verbally instructed during heelwork or could be from a static situation.

Principal observation

- Owner concentrating on the dog's response.

Stage Seven (Heelwork) – Training Element 3 (c)

EQUIPMENT

- Collar
- Lead
- Toys/titbits (if required)

TARGET

At the end of this stage the dog will be able to carry out loose lead walking after starting from an attentive sit position at the owner's left side. Minimum of encouragement should now be given during the loose lead walking process.

PRINCIPAL ACTIVITY AND HANDLING TECHNIQUE

(Accomplish Element 4 (c) before commencement of this routine)

The dog has already been taught to sit at the owner's left side for the Sit and Stay exercise; this is now incorporated into the start of the loose lead walking routine. Whilst on the lead, the dog should be instructed to sit at the owner's left side. The owner should step forward smartly with his left foot as he calls the dog's name with urgency. After that single step the owner should turn round and continue in the same direction but backwards and facing his dog, also encouraging him to catch up as quickly as possible. The same principal can be applied if the dog is found to lack enthusiasm and starts lagging behind.

Encouragement, inducement and if necessary a short sharp jerk on the lead may initially be required to obtain instant action from the dog. When the dog is moving at an attentive pace, with all the inducements necessary, the owner can again turn to continue forward in the same direction: three or up to ten paces backwards should be sufficient to achieve a satisfactory canine response.

As the dog learns the routine the backward movement can be minimised until it can be eliminated. At this time the dog should be prepared to move in time with the call of his name and the owner's first step forward.

This group makes up a sequence of movements for a single function of owner maintaining the same direction and changes from forward to backward movement and again to forward to counter a sluggish dog.

Activity Dog has a slow start or has been sluggish in movement.

Principal observation

- With the owner turning from walking forward to backward to entice and encourage the dog.

Activity Owner continues in the same direction but is moving backwards to generate more enthusiasm.

Principal observation

- With the owner walking backwards the dog is responding to the change of tact and with his own obvious enthusiasm.

Activity Owner again about turns to continue moving forward in the same direction with dog correctly and enthusiastically positioned at heel.

Principal observation

- Eye contact between owner and dog has been achieved and is being maintained.

- This activity has owner and dog working as a contented partnership.

Stage Eight (Heelwork) – Training Element 3 (d)

EQUIPMENT
- Collar
- Lead
- Short trailing line and activity cord
- Toys/titbits (if required)

TARGET

At the end of this stage the dog will be able to carry out halt and sit along with attentive right about turns with the dog maintaining position during the full turn. This is carried out in conjunction with the progress achieved through the Attention Generating routines. This can initially be on lead and, if advisable, followed by the short trailing line or the activity cord, then to be free from any attachment. It should now be possible to apply the minimum amount of encouragement and any titbits or toys to be introduced on completion along with generous praise for the dog's full and enthusiastic cooperation.

PRINCIPAL ACTIVITY AND HANDLING TECHNIQUE

Although sharp about turns may not be considered as a requirement for the pet dog owner the smart application of this movement is the sign of an attentive dog. The dog's expected response is similar to that of a sudden backward movement of the owner that follows a forward movement of both dog and owner as applied in target 1 (c) of the attention generating routine. As the owner about turns the dog is expected to maintain position with his head in line with the owner's left hand.

During a forward movement, with the dog carrying out attentive loose lead walking the owner, to give a special warning, uses the dog's name urgently as he moves backwards quickly to achieve a smart dog turn around. This movement may initially take about five backward paces in the direction of intended forward movement to ensure that the dog is maintaining an attentive attitude, the owner should then turn but continue in the same direction and encourage the dog to catch up as quickly as possible to maintain his position at the owner's left side. This is similar to the technique developed in stage 3 (c).

As the dog learns the routine, the backwards movement can be minimised and then eliminated as the owner turns on the spot with the dog maintaining the heel position and the owner makes a complete right about turn to move forward along the route he has just taken.

Activity Dog sitting while walking to heel with the short trailing line attached.

Principal observation

- Again the owner's watchful eye ensuring that the dog sits promptly when she halts.

Activity This group makes up a sequence of movements for the about turn and with the dog free of any attachments.

Principal observations

- Owner keeping an eye on her dog as she thinks about making the turn.

- The dog turns nicely behind the owner.

- The dog's body curls round the owner's legs to maintain close proximity as the owner prepares to step forward for the completion of the turn.

- Completion of the about turn with the dog walking nicely by the owner's left side.

Section 4

SIT AND STAY

Starting at Stage one from the Master Training Schedule (page 91)

EQUIPMENT – Training Element 4 (a)

- Collar
- Lead
- Toys/titbits (if required)

TARGET

At the end of this stage the dog will be able to stay sitting when put into that position by the owner. The owner should then stand straddled over the dog while both are facing the same direction to ensure that the dog does not move.

Note: With small dogs it may be more convenient for the owner to kneel with the dog positioned between the owner's knees.

PRINCIPAL ACTIVITY AND HANDLING TECHNIQUE

The approach to this target is to have the dog sit promptly and attentively at the owner's left hand side before he stands straddled over his dog. The owner should start with the dog on the lead and standing or moving by his left side.

The owner to take the lead in his right hand as close to the dog's collar as possible and at the same time to put his left hand at the left side of the dog's croup. To then push his rear end down and to the right as the owner's hand creates or maintains strict control of the lead. This double action should be carried out with co-ordination and purpose.

As this function is being carried out the owner should talk attentively, by giving a positive sit instruction to his dog as he is going into the sit.

Immediately the dog is in the sit position the owner should stand straddled over him with his hands stroking the dog's neck to give him reassurance and also to be ready to prevent the dog from changing his position, either to stand up or to lie down. The dog should be praised for staying in this position, and the owner must remain attentive to prevent the dog from moving.

Initially a five second stay in this position is quite sufficient before giving the dog freedom. It should be noted that by giving the dog freedom to break from the stay position this should just be as positive as the instruction to sit. At no time should the dog be allowed to move without full and enthusiastic permission from the owner.

Activity Putting a medium sized dog into the sitting position.

Principal observations

- Right hand controls head at the collar.
- Left hand at the groin applies pressure to ensure a prompt sit.

- The same principals apply with a small dog, but the owner must get down to the dog's level.

Activity Standing straddled behind a medium sized dog for the Sit and Stay. Also kneeling for a small dog.

Principal observations

- Owner's legs can start by being in contact with the dog, but at later stages the legs should be far enough apart to avoid body contact.

- Owner's hands can give comfort to the dog and are also ready to prevent any change in position from the dog. Owner's hands can also break contact with the dog, but be ready for action when required.

- It is important in the early stages that the owner gets down into the kneeling position with a small dog. Otherwise proper control cannot be maintained.

Stage Two (Sit and Stay) – Training Element 4 (b)

EQUIPMENT

- Collar
- Lead
- Toys/titbits (if required)

TARGET

At the end of this stage the dog will be able to stay in the sit position for at least ten seconds while the owner stands in front of him, or on occasions will walk round the dog at the end of a loose lead. At no time should the dog move from the sit until instructed.

PRINCIPAL ACTIVITY AND HANDLING TECHNIQUE

Before progressing from the straddled position the owner should ensure that his dog will accept gentle to enthusiastic praise without moving while he remains in a position to prevent such canine movement. Progress can be made when the dog accepts this enthusiastic praise without showing any intention of movement.

With the lead in hand the owner can then break contact with the dog by taking half a step backwards and keeping his feet well apart so that he is still in a position to anticipate canine movement and react accordingly. During the training for this target the lead must be kept loose as the owner starts to move round the dog, while using gentle praise and firm but quiet instructions to stay. Any canine movement must still be anticipated and prevented before any initial movement has resulted in a partial to complete change in position – into the stand or to lie down.

The owner should eventually be able to stand still, quietly, but very attentively in front of the dog at the end of a loose lead for a full ten seconds without any indication of canine movement.

Activity Inducing a dog into the sit position.

Principal observation

- Hands, body movement and voice are the inducements for the dog to sit.

- Although the lead is usually held in the right hand it is natural for an owner to change hands for giving signals of instruction or inducement to the dog.

Activity Inducing a large dog to sit.

Principal observation

- With a large dog it can be difficult to apply the normal approach and any (non cruel) inducement that works should be applied.

- Particularly with large dogs, training that includes manhandling of a dog should be carried out while the dog is of such a size and strength that it can be easily handled by the owner.

Stage Three (Sit and Stay) – Training Element 4 (c)

EQUIPMENT
- Collar
- Lead
- Toys/titbits (if required)

TARGET
At the end of this stage the dog will be able to sit immediately he is given verbal instruction while he is at the owner's left side. This should be carried out without any physical assistance.

PRINCIPAL ACTIVITY AND HANDLING TECHNIQUE
This is principally a stage that confirms the effect of positive sit training from the earlier targets. The dog should now be sitting immediately on the verbal instruction from the owner. The assistance of visual signals such as body, arm or hand movements, or the use of titbits to induce the appropriate response is quite permissible and is encouraged to ensure an immediate response.

Response must be attained on the first instruction although this instruction should be preceded by the use of the dog's name as an attention generator.

Praise is important for the consolidation of a good stay. Giving a build up of praise while the owner is in a position to prevent canine movement is a vital part of stay training.

Activity Inducing with a titbit to sit at the owner's left side.

Principal observation
- Position of the owner's hand with the titbit drawsthe dog into a nice close sit position.

Stage Four (Sit and Stay) – Training Element 4 (d)

EQUIPMENT

- Collar
- Lead
- Toys/titbits (if required)

TARGET

The dog to sit and stay at any time he is instructed within a reasonable distance from the owner. This will probably be about a lead length from the owner.

PRINCIPAL ACTIVITY AND HANDLING TECHNIQUE

With the dog on the lead but in a free standing or walking situation the owner should call his dog's name to obtain his attention and immediately move to stand at the dog's right side. He should maintain the dog's attention, then give the instruction to sit. Visual signals may also be initially given.

The owner then gradually minimises his movement until the dog responds to the sit instruction immediately after the first call of his name.

The maintained stay position should be continued for ten seconds while the owner moves round and stands at the dog's right side before giving his release.

Again praise along with positive control for sitting and staying in the elected position (sitting) is very important. The build up of praise without movement from the dog is the centre-pin for a consistently steady sit and stay within any situation.

Activity Owner has instructed the dog to stay in the sit position while she starts to walk round the dog.

Principal observation

- Owner's left hand is holding the lead in a manner that controls the dog from behind while she moves round the dog. Also giving verbal instruction to stay in the desired position.

Stage Five (Sit and Stay) – Training Element 4 (e)

EQUIPMENT

- Collar
- Lead
- Toys/titbits (if required)

TARGET

At the end of this stage the dog will be able to stay sitting for some thirty seconds while the owner is standing in various positions a lead length away. He must also remain sitting on return of the owner and until he is verbally released.

PRINCIPAL ACTIVITY AND HANDLING TECHNIQUE

This is an extension of target 4 (b) by building up on time along with distance away from the dog's side. Gentle praise can be given with visual signals to stay. The intermittent gentle but firm instruction to stay can also be given.

When the dog is well settled and the owner is confident that the dog will not move he can drop the lead, but move round or stand still within the appropriate distance from the dog.

A continuous watch must be kept on the dog during the whole period. When thirty seconds is achieved with no sign of canine movement short periods of silence, some five seconds or so, can be utilised to test the dog's reaction to inactivity.

The owner must be fully observant and be prepared for any thought of canine movement which would take the dog from the sit position. Any such thought must be countered before the dog actually changes from the sit position by giving positive instructioins to the dog to 'stay'.

A dog that occasionally or continually breaks from the sit stay during this time scale has not received the correct and full foundation during the earlier stages and a return to these earlier instructions is essential. The previous target was one of building up on time away from the dog. The objective is now to extend the period of time.

Through this sequence of training it is preferable that the owner moves backwards so that the dog can be watched the whole time. However, when confidence has been gained the owner may turn with his back to the dog to take a step or two to the end of the lead. Movement at a normal pace is initially preferable to sudden movements which may create the desire within the dog to move. The target is achieved when the owner can leave the dog at the sit and with the instruction to stay as he leaves his dog for that thirty second period. The owner may use verbal and visual aids to ensure a steady sit stay situation.

Activity Owner concentrating on ensuring the dog stays sitting while standing a lead length away from the dog.

Principal observation

- Flat of the hand being used to help maintain stable situation.

Stage Six (Sit and Stay) – Training Element 4 (f)

EQUIPMENT

- Collar
- Lead
- Toys/titbits (if required)

TARGET

At the end of this stage the dog will be able to remain sitting while the owner walks away for about ten paces in front of the dog, faces him for a full ten seconds or so then returns to his dog.

PRINCIPAL ACTIVITY AND HANDLING TECHNIQUES

The previous target was one of building up on time away from the dog. The objective is now to build up on distance.

Through a sequence of training sessions a pace or two further from the dog can be built up by taking time to move further away. It is preferable that the owner moves backwards so that the dog can be watched the whole time. When sufficient confidence has been gained the owner may turn and take a step or two with a full three hundred and sixty degree turn so that his back is to the dog for a very short moment at a time. Movement at a normal pace is preferable to quick movements at this time. These quick movements at an early stage may create the desire within the dog to move and could ruin progress to date. Situations with the owner's back to the dog can be extended as training progresses

The target is achieved when the owner can leave the dog at the sit and with the instruction to stay as he steps away smartly, walks out ten paces, turns to face his dog and remains there for ten seconds or so before returning smartly. The owner is encouraged to use verbal and visual aids to ensure a steady sit stay situation.

Stages Seven and Eight (Sit and Stay) – Training Element 4 (g)

EQUIPMENT

- Collar
- Lead
- Toys/titbits (if required)

TARGET

At the end of this stage the dog will be able to remain sitting while the owner walks away for a distance that builds up to twenty paces and duration of up to one minute. The dog should also remain sitting on return of the owner until he is released.

PRINCIPAL ACTIVITY AND HANDLING TECHNIQUE

The objective is now to build up on both time and distance to create a sound and controlled response from the dog. The general approach that was applied in the previous target is continued until both distance and time away from the dog meet the objectives of the target. Again verbal and visual aids should be utilised by the owner to maintain the success of previous targets. The owner must be fully observant and be prepared for the indications of any canine movement that is likely to take the dog from the sit position.

Any indication must be countered before the dog has actually changed from the sit stay to a stand or a down position by verbal and/or visual instructions to the dog to 'stay'.

A dog that continually breaks from the sit stay has not received the correct and full foundation during the earlier stages.

The prevention of failure and praise for success are important features for this and all other training procedures.

Section 5

DOWN AND STAY

Starting at stage two from the Master Training Schedule (page 91)

EQUIPMENT – Training Element 5 (a)

- Collar
- Lead
- Toys/titbits (if required)

TARGET

At the end of this stage the dog should be able to stay lying down when put into that position by the owner. The owner can kneel beside the dog to ensure that he does not move.

PRINCIPAL ACTIVITY AND HANDLING TECHNIQUES

At this stage the dog will be accustomed to being put into the sit position and it is best to use this as a basis for going into the down. Two approaches can be applied and it depends on the dog's reaction whether only one or both can be utilised.

1. With the dog in the sitting position the owner can entice the dog into the down by drawing his hand down to ground level with the use of titbits. Some dogs will find it natural to go into the down so that they can be given the titbit as a reward when they have reached the down position, and with their head at ground level. Other dogs will stand up, or raise their back end as the front end goes down. These dogs are not ready for this approach but may well respond at a later date after a more positive approach has been applied.

2. The more positive approach is to have the owner kneel at the dog's right side, put his left arm over the dog's shoulder to hold the dog's left front leg at the pastern. At the same time the owner's right hand holds the dog's front right leg at the pastern. The owner then lifts both front feet forward and drops his own body over the dog to ensure that the dog lies down and stays in that position.

With both approaches the instruction to go down can be gently but firmly given as the dog is going into the desired position. This should be immediately followed with gentle praise while the owner is in a position to prevent the dog from moving.

The dog should be kept in the down position for some twenty to thirty seconds before being enthusiastically and purposefully released.

Activity Inducing a dog into the down position.

Principal observation

The placing of the titbit in front of the dog's nose to draw her into the down position.

Activity Another inducment for a dog to go down.

Principal observations

- Drawing titbit under the bent knee to induce the dog down.

- Drawing a dog under a chair can serve the same purpose.

Activity Putting a dog into the down position.

Principal observations

- Owner kneeling close to dog.

- Owner lifts both front feet so that the dog's body can drop to the ground.

- When the dog is relatively large compared with the owner there can be difficulty in getting the left arm over the dog and to grasp the dog's left leg. This is a situation that can cause problems with this technique.

Stage Three (Down and Stay) – Training Element 5 (b)

EQUIPMENT
- Collar
- Lead
- Toys/titbits (not recommended until completion of that session of training)

TARGET
At the end of this stage the dog should be able to stay in the down position for at least ten seconds while the owner stands in front of him, or on occasion walks round the dog at the end of a loose lead.

PRINCIPAL ACTIVITY AND HANDLING TECHNIQUE
Before progressing from the kneeling position the owner should ensure that the dog accepts gentle enthusiastic praise without moving while he, the owner, is in a position to prevent such movement. Progress is made when the dog accepts this praise without showing any intention of moving.

With the lead in hand the owner can then break contact with the dog and kneel or sit some two feet away from him, but still watch for and anticipate canine movement, also to react before movement has taken place.

The owner can then stand up and move round his dog giving gentle praise along with the intermittent instruction to stay. The lead should be kept loose, whether the owner is standing or moving round the dog, any canine movement must be anticipated and caught before any initial movement has resulted in a change in position.

The objective of this target is achieved when the owner can stand in front of the dog at the end of a loose lead for fully ten seconds without any indication of canine movement. The ideal is to have the dog completely relaxed, but with that sense of responsibility.

Activity Down and stay position.

Principal observations

- Owner maintaining an attentive approach to ensure that the dog does not move as he walks round him.

- Note the flat of the hand being used as a 'barrier' and the dog's attention to the 'barrier'.

Stage Four (Down and Stay) – Training Element 5 (c)

EQUIPMENT

- Collar
- Lead
- Toys/titbits (not recommended until completion of that session of training)

TARGET

At the end of this stage the dog should be able to go down from the sit position immediately he is given the instruction. This should be carried out without physical assistance.

PRINCIPAL ACTIVITY AND HANDLING TECHNIQUE

At this stage the dog should sit when instructed without any physical assistance. This is now a continuation of the process and a quick owner movement to indicate the down position along with the verbal instruction will confirm the effect of the earlier targets. The use of titbits, verbal and visual aids are quite in order so long as the dog responds immediately and to the owner's initial instruction to go down.

The need for repeated instructions indicates insufficient grounding at the previous targets.

Activity Down and stay position by verbal and visual instructions.

Principal observations

- Owner bending bodily with finger indication to the dog to go down.

Stage Five (Down and Stay) – Training Element 5 (d)

EQUIPMENT

- Collar
- Lead
- Toys/titbits (not recommended until completion of that session of training)

TARGET

(Accomplish 4 (d) before commencement.)
At the end of this stage the dog should, within the lead length from the owner, be able to go down from the stand or sit at any time he is instructed.

PRINCIPAL ACTIVITY AND HANDLING TECHNIQUE

Having carried out the training to achieve target 4 (d) the dog is prepared to sit when instructed with the owner a lead length from the dog. A repeat of the process is carried out in achieving the down from a sit position.

Immediately after achieving a sit when instructed at a lead length away the owner should move towards the dog as he instructs the dog to go down while he gives visual and verbal encouragement.

A continuation of the practice will create the situation where the owner can minimise his movement towards the dog to achieve the desired result. The owner should maintain a firm down stay with his dog for ten seconds or so while the owner moves round at the end of a loose lead. He finally stands at the dog's right side before he releases him.

Stage Six (Down and Stay) – Training Element 5 (e)

EQUIPMENT

- Collar
- Lead
- Toys/titbits (not recommended until completion of that session of training)

TARGET

At the end of this stage the dog should be able to stay in the down position while the owner stands in various positions a lead length away for some thirty seconds. The dog must also remain down on return of the owner until released.

PRINCIPAL ACTIVITY AND HANDLING TECHNIQUE

This is an extension of target 5 (d) by building up on time away from the dog's side. Gentle praise can be given with visual signals to stay. The intermittent gentle but firm verbal instruction to stay can also be given. When the dog is nicely settled and the owner is confident the dog will not move from the down position he can drop the lead; but he can move round or stand still within the appropriate distance from the dog.

A continuous watch must be kept on the dog during the whole period. When thirty seconds is achieved with full canine contentment short periods of silence, some five seconds or so, can be utilised to test the dog's reaction to complete inactivity from the owner.

The owner must be fully observant and be prepared for any canine movement that will take the dog from the down position.

This must be countered before the dog actually changes from the down stay to the sit and stand by instructing the dog to 'stay'.

A dog which continually breaks from the down stay has not received the correct and full foundation during the early stages.

Stage Seven (Down and Stay) – Training Element 5 (f)

EQUIPMENT

- Collar
- Lead
- Toys/titbits (not recommended until completion of that session of training)

TARGET

At the end of this stage the dog should be able to remain down while the owner walks away for distances up to ten paces in front of his dog, faces him for one minute or so then returns to the dog.

PRINCIPAL ACTIVITY AND HANDLING TECHNIQUE

The previous target was one of building up on time away from the dog. The objective is now to build up on distance.

Through a sequence of training sessions a pace or two further away from the dog can be built up by taking time to move further away. It is preferable that the owner moves backwards so that the dog can be watched the whole time. When confidence has been gained the owner may turn and take a step or two with his back to the dog. Owner movement at a normal pace is preferable to quick movements that may create the dog's desire to move.

The target is achieved when the owner can leave the dog at the down and with the instruction to stay as he steps away smartly, walks ten paces, turns

to face his dog and remains there for one minute or so before returning smartly. The owner may use verbal and visual aids to ensure a steady down stay position.

Activity Owner maintaining the 'down' position.

Principal observations

- Owner concentrating on his dog while he is walking away to create a distance between himself and his dog.

- Note the flat of the hand as a 'barrier' and the attentiveness of the dog.

Stage Eight (Down and Stay) – Training Element 5 (g)

EQUIPMENT

- Collar
- Lead
- Toys/titbits (not recommended until completion of that session of training)

TARGET

At the end of this stage the dog should be able to remain down while the owner walks away for distances up to twenty paces and of up to two minutes duration.

PRINCIPAL ACTIVITY AND HANDLING TECHNIQUE

The objective is now to build upon both time and distance to create a sound and controlled response from the dog. The general approach, which was applied in the previous target, is continued until both distance and time away from the dog meet the objectives of the target. Again verbal and visual aids along with praise while the dog is staying should be utilised by the owner to maintain the success of the previous target.

The owner must be fully observant and be prepared for any canine movement that could take the dog from the down position.

This must be countered before the dog has actually changed from the down stay to the sit or stand by instructing him to 'stay'. A dog that continually breaks from the down stay has not received the correct and full foundation during the earlier stages.

Section 6

STAY STANDING

Starting at stages five and six from the Master Training Schedule (page 91)

EQUIPMENT – Training Element 6 (a)

- Collar
- Lead
- Long trailing line
- Toys/titbits (not recommended until completion of that session of training)

TARGET

(Accomplish 1 (b) before commencement)
At the end of this stage the dog should be able to stay standing at the end of a loose lead and without moving forward while there are minor through moderate to major distractions in front of him, five to ten seconds of time is all that is required.

PRINCIPAL ACTIVITY AND HANDLING TECHNIQUE

An introduction to the attention generating routine at target 1 (b) is preferable and will make this exercise much easier to attain. Training at this stage is again with the dog on the lead.

From the start it can be more effective to make use of distractions and these can be in the form of a relative or friend that the dog wants to go and see. It may be the sight of another dog some distance away or it may just be the desire to go out for a walk which creates the desire to pull on the lead. Training is best carried out when these natural situations arise.

A firm voice and a positive lead action are the principal controlling features, but a stamp of the foot to maintain attention can also be effective.

When the owner wishes to have the dog stay and stand he should have his name called by a friend as he physically prevents the dog from moving forward on the lead. In extreme circumstances it may be necessary to apply a jerk on the end of the lead with the degree of force required. It is important to apply, with timing, the use of the voice to give the instruction to stay. When working against any degree of distraction too much verbal or physical force could create an immediate return of the dog to owner. This is likely to be due to the effectiveness of attention generating training already accomplished. Strict instructions to the dog are a must with all stay training and must be tempered by praise for a satisfactory reaction. The dog can maintain his attention on the cause of his desire to pull on the lead, but as a result of the owner's action the dog should *always* remain stationary.

Any attempt from the dog to take a step forward to be countered by further instructions to stay, tension on the lead, or if it is absolutely necessary, that little jerk. When the dog can stay for some five to ten seconds without the tension on the lead and allows the owner to step forward to his side without any attempt to move indicates that the target has been achieved.

A long trailing line can also now be used instead of the lead where the owner can stand on the line or pick it up as desired and use it as an extended lead; but to take the line in by hand to make sure that the dog does not move forward towards the distraction.

Praise for staying and an official break from the stay should complete any training stint and can be immediately followed by, fun, games, or/and titbit to show the great pleasure and appreciation of the owner.

Activity Physically preventing dogs from moving forward.

Principal observation

At this stage the owners are preventing the dogs from moving towards a distraction. The tension on the lead and the line will not be released until the dogs are prepared to stay by verbal instructions only.

Stages Seven and Eight (Stay Standing) – Training Element 6 (b)

EQUIPMENT

- Collar
- Lead
- Toys/titbits (not recommended until completion of that session of training)

TARGET

At the end of this stage the dog should be able to stay standing and without moving forward at a distance of up to ten paces from the owner. The dog can be facing the owner or a distraction in some other direction and should be standing until approached by the owner for the lead to be attached.

PRINCIPAL ACTIVITY AND HANDLING TECHNIQUE

A continuation from target 6 (a) should allow the owner to apply verbal instructions to stay whilst the dog is off the lead but, initially, within a pace or two from the dog. The owner giving a stamp of his foot can also be effective in getting home to the dog that he should be paying attention. These actions should initially be carried out while there are no obvious distractions to take the dog away. The owner should finish by going to the dog to give praise.

Development can take place with a gradual increase of distances until ten paces between dog and owner and with the evidence of distractions. A gradual increase in distance and a reasonable approach to the magnitude of distractions should not be difficult to accomplish.

It should be recognised that it can be very difficult to stop a dog that is actually running away, particularly when there is a distraction that has become a strong objective in the mind of the dog. It is preferable not to call a dog rather than court failure by having him ignore a call to stop. In circumstances like this the owner must accept responsibility for allowing the situation to develop.

Activity Maintaining the stay standing from a short distance.

Principal observation

- The use of the flat of the hand along with verbal instructions to stay.

The owner should observe his own activities when a distracted dog is likely to run away. Most dogs will look at the distraction for a second or so before determining their course of action. It should be recognised that dogs rarely 'run away' from their owners, unless through fear. However, unless controlled, they may well run to an interesting distraction. Under conditions like stand and stay, training can be much more effective than trying to recall.

I will end by reiterating what I wrote at the start of this chapter, namely that although the training described for the basic objectives does not take the owner through to a higher level of training for competitive standards the approach gives a solid foundation for each of the six exercises as applied where the owner's particular requirements are much more demanding.

Chapter 14

DEVELOPING ADVANCED ROUTINES

Advanced training routines require that the dog has a measure of basic control before the advanced work can commence. The measure of basic control depends on the exercise under consideration and also the knowledge and ability of the party training the dog.

While judging or just observing Obedience tests and Working trials over the years I have seen many mistakes being made in the execution of so many exercises. Most of these mistakes were due to failures within the training of the basic exercises described in Chapter 13. Getting it right within the basic exercises is essential and serious consideration is being given to the development into the field of advanced work, particularly if competitions or qualifications are in mind.

The advanced exercises, just like the basic, have to be broken down into their respective elements, be analysed for order of introduction and rate of progress. They also have to be modified if required to suit the particular circumstances. There may even, in the early stages, be the need to allow or encourage activities that are decidedly wrong in the long term to achieve the desired at some crucial stage in the training procedure.

I have also found when training my own dogs, but particularly when instructing others, that it is better to note but ignore some of the minor faults so that we may concentrate and obtain substantial progress with some of the more serious problems. The minor faults can be treated at a later date. It can have a negative effect to burden an owner with too many faults at a time that they require to be motivated by a measure of success and a bit of encouragement instead of continually putting problems in their way.

My objective within this chapter is to go through the development of one advanced exercise so that the reader can understand the process and develop his own approach to the same or other exercises. The chosen exercise is the Retrieve.

The previous chapter gives all the details for basic control.

Retrieving articles

The retrieving of articles is an essential requirement for various fields of competition, although the use of a dumbbell in a retrieve exercise along with many other types of article are utilised competitively. Training will initially be given with the most suitable articles. However the dumbbell will eventually play its part in the full procedure.

The ability to go out and bring back various types of articles is prominent within the requirements of Working trials and Obedience and it can also be very important in the part of daily life for any dog. One just has to watch the fun and games that dogs and their owners have by 'throw and fetch' and throw again. The retrieve can be of value to create versatility in the ability to retrieve different articles.

PRELIMINARY TRAINING

Much of the training requires a good solid recall and any training for a retrieve should take this into account. Although both recall and retrieve can be trained in parallel, it is important to recognise that many retrieve problems are due to inadequacies in the training for the recall or the failure to achieve a basic 'come back when called' domestic requirement.

AN UNDERSTANDING OF DOGS

To pick up and carry an article is the most natural act for any dog, although no doubt there will be one or two dogs that will prove me wrong. There will be owners of other dogs who will consider that their dogs have no natural ability to pick up and carry, but this failure is often due to some factor within the dog's environment during part of his life.

However, it should be recognised that there are various factors within a dog's genetic make up that can affect his ability to conform to his owner's requirements. It is well known that the working gun dogs have been bred particularly with retrieving in mind, while with many other breeds the ability to retrieve is of no importance. Therefore, there is bound to be a great variety of natural ability.

It is easy to develop retrieving faults and, at times, difficult to appreciate their existence until they have a good hold. However, the full understanding of the retrieve is held within the Retrieve Matrix.

There are natural and environmental weaknesses and strengths that make a difference to training. The two most important are the possessive and submissive traits. Possessiveness is very helpful, but if the trait is too strong, there can be difficulties getting a dog to come back and release the article.

Submissiveness that is too strong may affect a dog's ability to leave the owner and go out to retrieve. A weakness within this trait can result in dominance and the difficulty to control a dog's actions. It should also be assessed as to whether the traits are natural or manmade.

Each dog has his natural level of either trait, from very strong in some dogs to very weak in others. It is the combination of these strengths or weaknesses that govern our progress in retrieve training.

A strong possessive trait should result in a dog having a very keen natural desire to go after a suitable toy or article. However, a dog that is weak in this trait will require to be suitably induced to realise the pleasures of controlled possessiveness.

A strong submissive trait will result in an easy recall, unless unsympathetic handling has created apprehension or fear and the negation of a natural response. A weak submissive trait will undoubtedly result in a very independent dog unless this factor has been properly controlled.

THE RETRIEVE MATRIX

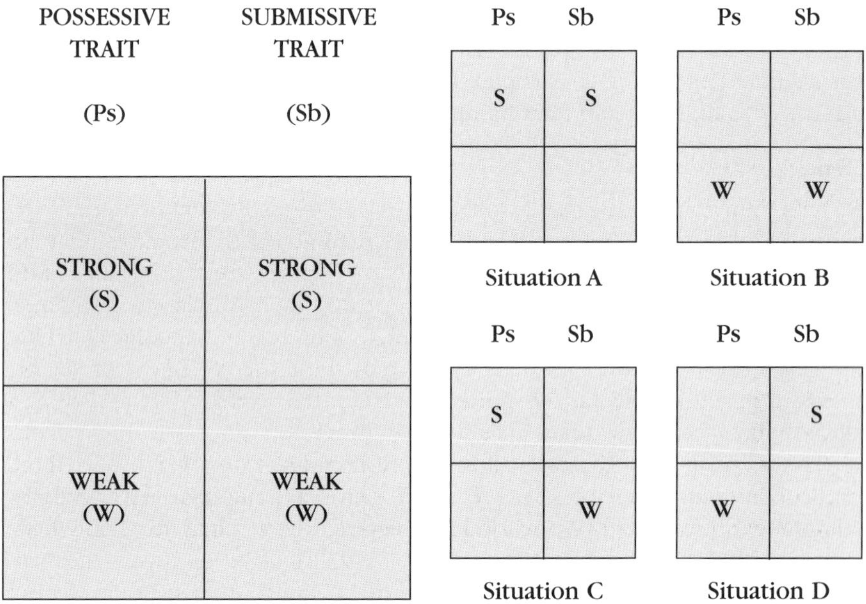

Figure 1 – **Retrive Matrix**

Therefore, we have four combinations within the Matrix to give us a variety of basic training situations utilising both the Possessive and the Submissive traits (see above).

Situation A

The combination of two strong traits creates the easiest training conditions where the strong possessive trait ensures a natural desire to go out and take possession of the article and the strong submissive trait ensures an immediate return on the call.

Situation B

Here we have a dog with no desire to go out for the article and when he has been induced to go out will become too independent to return unless the owner has overcome the 'conflict of interests' situation. This combination of two weak traits will create a situation where great patience will be required with the timing and introduction of each training element being controlled to assure success.

Situation C

The strength of possessiveness will achieve an enthusiastic run out for the article and simplify the initial training, but the problems in handling the uncontrolled independent dog require to be tackled and cured before any further progress can be made. The failure to recognise this situation is often witnessed when a dog can be seen to run out for a thrown article and then run away to find his own form of amusement with his 'toy'.

Situation D

As with Situation B the initial problem is to build up sufficient enthusiasm to carry the dog through the more difficult retrieve-based exercises that lie ahead. The time and effort put into a weak possessive trait will be well rewarded by the ease in which the strong submissive trait will fall into place.

The problems we see regularly with dogs who refuse to retrieve or play up when they pick up their article, are generally due to a lack of understanding by the owner of the principal canine traits which affect his dog's attitude to this exercise.

The strengths or weaknesses of these principal traits may well be inherited, but the environment can influence the situation enormously. A young dog who spent an extended puppyhood in breeding kennels may not know how to enjoy the fun and games that can be had with toys of his own, especially when the owner is not prepared to play with him. A forced method of hold and carry used in the early stages of training can also give the impression of weakness instead of a strong possessive trait. There can be many manmade reasons for failing to achieve a happy and responsive retrieving dog.

Manmade reasons for retrieving failures can be more difficult and time consuming to rectify than a straightforward programme used to train a dog from scratch.

EQUIPMENT

If the dog is wearing a slip collar, the dead ring can be used as an attachment of the lead to avoid the collar tightening on the dog's neck. A lead of about four to six feet in length may also be advisable for control in the earlier stages. The activity cord could be useful for the later stages; the cord should be about six feet in length with a handling loop at one end and the other end free to slip out of the dead ring on the collar when the end is dropped.

The most suitable article for initial training could be any or all of the following which are illustrated in Chapter 7.

A folded sock or a glove
A suitable soft toy
A length of plastic or rubber tubing that would eventually be slit and fitted over the centre of a dumbbell

Other types of articles and a dumbbell will be required at a later stage to create versatility for the various competitive exercises.

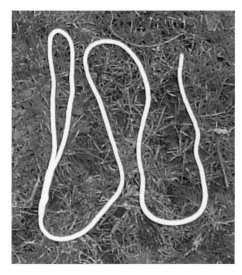

Activity cord.

I would not recommend the use of food as a reward for retrieving as this can encourage a dog to drop the article in anticipation of receiving the food. Greater effort should be made to apply a follow up activity by encouraging the dog to retake the article and apply enthusiastic personal approval (praise) from yourself.

When a satisfactory retrieve has been achieved, the training item used can be attached to the centre of the dumbbell so that a satisfactory transfer can be applied. If the toy being used is not suitable for attaching to a dumbbell the transfer to one of the other articles may be required before finally attaching the article to the dumbbell. Training with a dumbbell in the early stages of the retrieve is not advisable. The centre is relatively hard and any problems that can arise are likely to put the dog off retrieving a dumbbell for a long time (or for ever). It is preferable to use one of the recommended articles, or something similar; if a problem does arise it is easy to discard the 'offending' article and introduce a different one.

INFORMAL TRAINING

Informal training is applied when a youngster or older dog has the natural desire to 'pick up and carry'. A great deal can be done at an early stage to 'groom' youngsters to 'hold and carry', also to fetch as well. If a youngster, or an older untrained dog, is prepared to come to hand with a toy or some other article, always be prepared to show your pleasure, take it from him then give it back to him as a reward. Although this should be encouraged a number of problems can arise, such as:

1. Picking up and carrying round forbidden items, such as socks, slippers or underwear.
2. Destructiveness and mouthing.
3. Refusing to 'give to hand'.
4. Dropping the item in front of you.
5. Running away and hiding.

So many of these problems are caused by the owners (or family members) through their previous activities. Youngsters can be encouraged to be destructive by the owner thinking it is 'funny' to see their youngster destroying something of no value. Dogs or youngsters do not put a value on anything they pick up. On the other hand, they may have been forcibly discouraged from picking up or destroying a forbidden item. All possibilities should be recognised as a cause of a problem.

ELEMENTARY TRAINING

The avoidance of problems will do much to achieve a good sound retrieve as well as the understanding of a youngster's enjoyment. We should therefore have a training routine that gives consideration to the various problems to ensure that they can be minimised or avoided completely.

The elementary training to be described may not be successful with every dog, especially if a different approach has already created problems. Much depends on your own ability and involvement. However all dogs will benefit to a greater or lesser extent and will help to give both you and your dog fun and confidence. An alternative, but more demanding, but still 'kindly' approach is also included in this presentation. Firstly, there should be more than one retrieve article of a type available or a variety of such articles. One of my own favourites is a folded sock. This can be folded into a suitable size and stitched so that it does not unfold. To have three or four at hand could be very useful. If you have only the one, it is not unusual to find that it has been misplaced when you want it. Through the rest of this training procedure I shall write about the sock although you may chose something different. Your youngster should never be left to play or chew any of the chosen articles.

Folded sock.

145

Secondly, you should have some play toys or fun articles. These may include squeaky or soft toys, balls, plastic bottles or waxed paper cartons, whatever suits your dog, and if these items are destructible, they can easily be replaced. Your youngster, or older untrained dog can do as he pleases with these articles.

If your youngster takes a particular liking to one of these play toys and is happy to bring it to hand you may wish to take it out of the 'play toy' category and use it as your retrieve article. You should always be prepared to modify your approach if you can see a decided advantage without the creation of other problems.

There is an old saying that goes 'You don't have to be daft to train a dog, but it does help'; and this is the time to make it work in your favour. How you induce your youngster to pick up the sock is up to you, but make a game of it. You can throw or kick any of his toys around to create a game of it and, when he does pick it up, do not be too ready to take it from him unless he delivers it to hand, then you give it back to him. It can be fun to have a toy tied to the end of a piece of string so that you can drag it across the floor or you can create a flight impression. A very short tug of war with an item, and, him winning, can be helpful; but if the tension on the other end causes a problem just drop your end as soon as he has it in his mouth.

Any time he picks up anything and carries of his own volition, be it in the house, out in the garden or for a walk, give him encouragement. Tell him how clever he is. If he comes back to you with it, good, but do not ask him to do anything that is likely to cause a failure.

When you have 'come when called' training at a satisfactory level, you can then introduce this activity while he is actually carrying. When he comes to you do not make him sit, but take the article from him with great pleasure and reward him by giving it back. At this stage, his greatest reward is to see that you are happy and he gets his 'toy' back. He can then do what he wants with it. Each time you call him to you with a 'toy', show your pleasure, take it then give it back so that he can do as he wishes with it.

You can introduce the sock when your youngster is prepared to bring a toy to you when you ask for it. You can now do likewise with the sock. Kick, throw or tie it on the end of a piece of string, when he picks it up get him to you immediately, take it, show your pleasure and give it back. If he is going to carry it, let him for a few seconds then call him back and repeat the process. Two or three such recalls at a time are sufficient then replacing the sock with a play toy so that he can finish the session as he wishes. He should not be allowed to be destructive with your article, but it is all right with a toy.

The exercise – article retrieving

THE FULL OBJECTIVE

To have the dog, when instructed, go out, pick up and return with an article or a dumbbell he has watched the owner throw. On return, to sit in front of him, give to hand then return to heel.

This exercise covers or affects one or more exercises in the control group within Working trials or within the Obedience routines. The precision required is determined by the standards of the owner's chosen activity.

EQUIPMENT

- Collar
- Lead
- Activity cord and/or loop
- A folded sock, glove or some such article
- A suitable soft toy.
- An alternative is a length of plastic or rubber tubing that would eventually be slit and fitted over the centre bar of a dumbbell.

Note: Other types of articles and a dumbbell will be required at a later stage to create versatility for the various competitive exercises.

THE BASIC ELEMENTS

The dog to:

(a)   Sit at the owner's left side while the retrieve article is thrown.
(b)   After the owner has thrown the article the requisite distance and, and on the owner's instruction, dog to move out at a smart pace to pick up the article.
(c)   Turn and come back to the owner at a smart pace with the article firmly in his mouth.
(d)   On his return to sit relatively straight and close in front of the owner while he retains the article.
(e)   Allow the owner to take the article from his mouth.
(f)   Go round to sit at the owner's left side (to heel) on his instruction.
(g)   Remain sitting at heel until released.

Note: A number of these elements also relate to the competitive *recall* exercise and this should be trained ahead of and to the required standard before involving these elements in the retrieve training routine.

THE TRAINING PROCEDURE

Note: There can always be different approaches to carrying out a training routine and its documented presentation. The presentation of this training procedure differs slightly from those in Chapter 13 and the reader should always consider the approach that suits himself when developing a routine. In this instance, I have added an Objective as well as a Target because it is felt that the exercise justifies the change.

FIRST TARGET

At the end of this stage the dog should be willing to take and keep hold of the article.
Note: This is for dogs that have *not* introduced or adapted to the elementary training routine.

OBJECTIVE

Learning the routine for part of Elements (b) and (e) [as listed above] to take, hold and give the article back to the owner.

PRINCIPAL ACTIVITY AND HANDLING TECHNIQUES

Although some owners would prefer to start by using one of the soft articles already recommended, I shall start this routine by using the index finger without protection (such as a glove) as the training article. By recommending this approach excess pressure cannot be applied to the dog's mouth without hurting the owner's finger. This is a guarantee that the owner will not use excessive force and cannot hurt the dog

Any youngster or dog should become familiar with the index finger massaging his gums and be quite happy to accept the finger in his mouth. Any owner who cannot carry out this function without being bitten has a real behaviour problem on his hands.

With the dog or youngster sitting, the owner to straddle him so that they are both facing in the same direction and he should show affection by stroking the dog and then place the index finger behind his canines. With the thumb over his muzzle and remaining fingers under his lower jaw hold the dog's mouth shut. Give gentle praise, stroke his cheek or chest and ask him to 'Hold'. Restrict this action to about three or four seconds during the first few occasions. Do not overdo it and do not lengthen the holding periods until the dog is happy to accept this procedure.

The owner is always in a position to know if there is any loose skin from the upper or lower lips being caught between the finger and the dog's teeth and this should be cleared before applying any pressure. Any attempt to apply excessive pressure when holding the dog's muzzle will hurt the owner long before it has any effect on the dog. To remove the finger, release the grip over his muzzle and, as the dog opens his mouth to release the index finger, ask him to 'Give' as the finger is taken out by the front of his mouth. The finger goes in from the side but comes out by the front.

It will not take him long to realise that the index finger behind his canines is quite an acceptable experience and the dog will start to hold without any pressure being applied to keep his mouth shut. Each time the finger is put in his mouth use a gentle 'Hold' along with praise and gentle stroking. Make sure the experience becomes a pleasant one, but be ready to hold his mouth shut if he thinks of opening it before asking him to give the finger back.

When satisfied and perfectly happy with the dog's acceptance of this procedure prepare to teach him to carry the finger. Stand in front of the dog (he may be sitting or standing) and get him to hold the index finger again. With the thumb over his muzzle and the remaining fingers under his lower jaw the dog to be encouraged to follow as the owner walks backwards. Keep asking him to hold, encourage him, and on occasions pull against his canines but make sure he realises that he should not open his mouth. Let him release the finger only when you are ready and request it.

It is the sensitivity of his finger that prevents the owner from applying excess pressure when holding the dog's mouth shut. This ensures a gentle and considerate approach to the rudiments of retrieve training.

During this period of training, the owner is in a position to control the dog's actions. If he is going to reject the finger, the owner has the means of preventing it. The owner should be able to sense the dog's actions much quicker than by using some other object. The owner is in a position to comfort the dog by stroking his chest or cheeks and yet apply the correct amount of pressure as and when it is required with the knowledge that he is not being hurt.

Progress depends to a great extent on the owner's approach and the dog's readiness to accept his actions. This method can also be used to retrain dogs that have already been trained to retrieve, but have mouthing or dropping problems, or are reluctant to release the article.

The next stage is to use a suitable replacement for the index finger. Any one of the items listed under the heading of Equipment will do. Although some photos will depict other articles, this is where I shall designate a folded sock for convenience within the text. Again, it is preferable that the dog be straddled so that both dog and owner are facing the same direction and then put the sock in his mouth whilst asking him to hold it. Praise and stroking his chest or cheeks will help to dispel any anxiety. When using an article other than the finger it should go into the dog's mouth from the front, with the article initially being placed after opening the dog's mouth by using the thumb and index finger under the dog's lower jaw.

It will probably be found that he will accept the change of 'article' and prove that the groundwork with the index finger has been worthwhile. The owner should now stand in front of the dog and with one hand under his chin, get him to follow the owner as he is moving backwards. It will be realised by the owners of small dogs that they will need to get down to the dog's level and, instead of standing straddled over the dog, they may have to kneel. Dogs can respond much better when people are down to their level and some of the basic training with youngsters or small dogs can be carried out from the kneeling position. It is recognised that the backward movement when kneeling with a small dog can be rather restrictive.

Keep the training sessions short and make sure the dog does not get bored.

Activity Holding index finger.

Principal observations

- Owner inserts finger from the side and behind the canines.

- Right hand stroking the dog's chest.

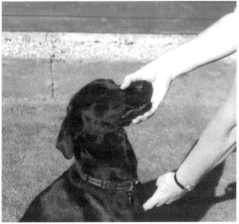

Activity Holding index finger when standing in front of the dog.

Principal observations

- Owner inserts index finger from the side and behind the canines.

- Left hand stroking the dog's chest.

Activity Holding soft article.

Principal Observations

- Owner keeping the lower jaw from dropping which would allow the dog to drop the article.

- It is important that the dog maintains a grip of the article.

SECOND TARGET

At the end of this stage the dog should be willing to move around carrying the article.

OBJECTIVE

Learning the routine for part of Element (c) and (e). To carry and come back at a smart pace holding the article firmly in his mouth, then willingly allow the owner to take the article.

PRINCIPAL ACTIVITY AND HANDLING TECHNIQUES

It should not take the dog long to realise there is great pleasure in strutting round with an article in his mouth.

When there is full confidence that he wants to walk around holding the article, the owner to run backwards and call him. Get him excited, but be prepared to use a firm verbal instruction to 'Hold' if the dog thinks of mouthing, chewing or even dropping the article. It may be desirable to carry out the initial part of this training whilst the dog is on the lead. With some dogs, the excitability may have to be toned down.

It is only when the dog holds with excitement that the owner can consider enticing him to take the article as he is being teased with it. Having carried this out successfully on a few occasions the article can be 'accidentally' dropped by the owner as he tries to grab it. During the excitement, the dog should be ready to pick up the article and carry it as he is induced into the recall while the owner is moving backwards and away from his dog.

This is a critical stage in the training programme and it is important that the dog picks up from the 'accidental' drop before progressing to the next stage.

The pick up should now be consolidated by dropping the article and on occasions by kicking it around to increase the dog's desire to get hold of it.

As he has been taught to hold and carry until the article is taken from him, there should not be any problems in getting him to present to hand although any excitement may have made the dog forget. If this happens it may be good policy to put him on the lead for a short spell to bring his mind back to the initial recall training element. Again, one hundred per cent success is required during any training session before considering instructions to go out and fetch.

THIRD TARGET

At the end of this stage the dog should be willing to move from the owner to pick up a thrown article.

OBJECTIVE

Learning the routine for another part of Element (b) and (e) (as listed on page 147) to fetch, hold and give the article back to the owner.

PRINCIPAL ACTIVITY AND HANDLING TECHNIQUES

The sight of the training article should now be sufficient to excite the dog and a short throw can be tried. At this stage, do not make him stay before throwing the article or make him sit on his return with it. The approach is still very informal. Dogs with a strong response to the recall may find the excitement of a longer throw more to their liking. As soon as the dog picks up the article, the owner to revert to the recall procedure as he moves backwards at a suitable pace to bring the dog back as fast as possible. Owners should always give sufficient room behind them for a lengthy backward movement if it is required.

Verbal instructions to 'Fetch it' are not necessary at this stage. It is the desire to get the article, which takes the dog out, and not the owner's instruction. The use of verbal instructions at this stage can result in a commanding voice that may put a dog off. When the verbal instruction is used, it should be in the form of an excited request rather than a formal command. The dog can then learn the meaning of the phrase 'Fetch it' after he knows how to perform the act. A command, instruction or request verbally given to a dog means nothing until he knows how to perform the act.

Owners should not be in too much of a hurry to take the article from the dog. The owner may have to put one hand under the dog's chin while the other is used to stroke him, probably his forehead.

When the owner is ready to take the article, he should take both hands and gently draw them across the dog's cheeks as he is spoken to nicely, he may be asked to keep a hold of the article. As the owner's hands reach the article, he takes it and asks the dog to 'give'.

He should get into the habit of using both hands to draw them across the dog's cheeks until the article is in both hands of the owner. The owner may wish to give the article back to the dog then repeat the process.

When the pick up, hold, carry and deliver to hand is to the owner's satisfaction the extended throw can be developed so that the dog will go out any distance to pick up and return to the owner.

FOURTH TARGET

At the end of this stage the dog should be willing to sit in front of the owner and deliver the article to hand.

OBJECTIVE

Learning the routine for Element (d). On returning to the owner the dog to sit in front, present the article to be taken by the owner.

PRINCIPAL ACTIVITY AND HANDLING TECHNIQUES

The dog now knows to run out and pick up a small variety of 'easy' articles and go back immediately to the owner when called, but to accommodate more of the competition requirements it is advisable that the training for the full competitive Recall exercise has been perfected.

The owner should now be interested in having his dog sit well in front of him before he accepts the article from the dog. As he has been taught to sit in front of the owner without an article in his mouth during Recall training, it should be quite easy to have him do it when instructed then to deliver the article to hand. If a little assistance is initially required, the owner should put a hand under the dog's lower jaw as it is drawn up while instructing him to 'sit'. Note that, to release the article the dog would have to lower his jaw and by the simple action of a hand under the jaw a number of problems can be avoided.

After taking the article and praising him, the normal element of 'round to heel' to finish the exercise is applied.

After the owner takes the article, it will help the dog's confidence to have it given back to him. The owner to apply a little fondling and praise before finally taking the article on completion of that part of the training session.

Activity Owner placing his hands behind the article so that he may stroke the dog and he should be prepared to take the article when ready.

Principal observation

- Owner using both hands to stroke the dog's neck and be ready to prevent the dog from dropping the article. This helps to create a pleasant atmosphere and prevents the owner from making a 'grab' for the article.

Activity A continuation of above activity.

Principal observation

- While drawing the hands forward, the owner holds the article (in this instance, a dumbbell) to remove it gently from the dog's mouth with the request 'Give'.

FIFTH TARGET

At the end of this stage the dog should be willing to sit at the left side of the owner while the article is thrown and he should wait for the instruction to go out and retrieve.

OBJECTIVE

Learning the routine for Element (a) and (b). To sit and wait at the owner's side and to go out for the article when released.

PRINCIPAL ACTIVITY AND HANDLING TECHNIQUES

The final element now required to complete the retrieve exercise is to teach the dog to sit by the owner's left hand side and wait for the release to go out for the thrown article. The owner's attitude to date has been to create enthusiasm and anticipation, the dog has been allowed to run free when the article has been thrown, now the owner wants to have the dog wait for the word to go. It is now preferable to curb his anticipation without adversely affecting his enthusiasm.

Physical restraint is now necessary. Hold his collar while throwing his article out. Keep him back for a few seconds before releasing him with the verbal request to 'fetch it'. When you are sure that none of the enthusiasm is lost, in fact, it may get stronger, make him sit and physically keep him sitting while the article is thrown out. Keep him sitting for a few seconds before releasing him with a very enthusiastic 'fetch it'.

When he has steadied down and is ready to wait for the release to go and fetch his article, make use of a short activity cord or loop and slip the end of the cord through the dead ring on his collar – it is preferable not to use the 'check' function of a slip collar. If the loop is used, it can be used in conjunction with the collar as a holding device when and as required. With the cord in place, hold both ends, and as with the loop, the dog will not know whether the owner can maintain physical control or not, until he thinks of making a break for his article. It may well be necessary to use strong verbal instructions to 'wait' until he is released with 'fetch it'. This will take time, but the perfecting of any exercise does take time and especially to counter the anticipation that has previously been encouraged. When he is released, keep hold of the loop end of the cord and drop the other end so that it slips out of the collar. If the loop is used, it can be released and left attached to the collar. Enthusiasm to retrieve has been created and can now be drawn on to achieve control. Like a lot of other exercises, enthusiasm and anticipation should be encouraged, then controlled.

Within the basic retrieving exercise, the dog should now be considered to be fully trained. This approach is advisable before developing to the more difficult articles that are required in the Sixth and Seventh Targets that follow.

SIXTH TARGET

At the end of this stage the dog should be willing to retrieve a dumbbell.

OBJECTIVE

Learning to retrieve a specific article for competitive purposes. One of the reasons for selecting the soft training article is its ability to be tied to the centre shaft of a dumbbell.

PRINCIPAL ACTIVITY AND HANDLING TECHNIQUES

It is time to go back to Third Stage and apply the informal training with the soft article tied to the centre bar of the dumbbell until the owner and his dog are happy to retrieve this combination. The training article can then be

removed and the dog should be happy to retrieve the dumbbell on its own.

The full exercise can now be accomplished without any trouble.

Activity A soft article tied to the centre bar of the dumbbell.

Principal observation

- Owner using both hands to stroke the dog and be ready to prevent the dog from dropping the dumb-bell. This helps to create a pleasant and pleasurable atmosphere for the dog.

SEVENTH TARGET

At the end of this stage the dog should be willing to retrieve a variety of articles.

OBJECTIVE

Learning to retrieve articles of a material, style or type that are more difficult for the dog.

PRINCIPAL ACTIVITY AND HANDLING TECHNIQUES

Again, return to the Third Stage, particularly with articles the dog is unlikely to find easy. There are various reasons why dogs find some articles particularly easy to pick up and others find them to be very difficult. A motor car spark plug, which is heavy for its size is one example, but this is where the enthusiasm that has been built into his performances creates an advantage.

With any such article, fun is the name of the game and a formal retrieve should be avoided with 'difficult' articles until the informal approach means that this type of article is no longer considered to be 'difficult'.

The retrieve can be carried out in a manner that suits the situation – be it for informal pleasure or the strictest of competitive circumstances.

Activity Presenting a throw ring to his owner.

Activity Two working trials Labradors working in tandem.

Principal observation

With both illustrations – the attentiveness of the dogs and owners.

Chapter 15

UNDERSTANDING COMPETENCE OF PERFORMANCE

The effect of any training programme is in the satisfaction of the owner and the dog, also an instructor, if involved. This satisfaction may be related to a degree of domestic competence or a level within the field of professional or competitive programmes.

It is not satisfaction that causes an owner's displeasure, but the degree of dissatisfaction caused by performances that are below par. When there is dissatisfaction the answers are related to *why* has it happened? And *what* can be done to improve the situation?

To help with the why and the what, there are a variety of approaches that can assist in solving the problems and create performance improvements. Four different approaches are being presented with any one or all having a place in the achievement of compliance to the desired standard. They are:

- Assessments of skills and methods.
- Developing an activity breakdown.
- Problem identification and analysis.
- Session instructional plan.

Assessments of skills and methods

This has been put in a format that can be used at any time and any stage of training to give an objective picture of the owner's approach to the particular subject. This can be constructive if a knowledgeable friend, or instructor at a training class, was to apply this form of evaluation as a whole, to cover single or selected sections of the assessment.

ASSESSMENTS OF SKILLS AND TRAINING METHODS

This is a practical approach to assessing the skills of an owner/dog relationship and the training methods being used by the partnership for any selected training exercise or an element of that exercise.

Selected Exercise/Element ⎯⎯⎯⎯⎯⎯⎯⎯⎯⎯⎯⎯⎯⎯⎯⎯⎯⎯

Owner/Dog Partnership ⎯⎯⎯⎯⎯⎯⎯⎯⎯⎯⎯⎯⎯⎯⎯⎯⎯⎯⎯

Areas of assessment

1. Equipment and its application   **COMMENTS**

    Collar type
    Lead – suitable material and length
    Cord (line) being used – suitable material and length
    Retractable lead
    Toys
    Titbits

2 Practical Workout

2.1   **Preparation**
    Application of equipment
    Dog motivation
    Owner's control over situation

2.2   **Basic forms of communication**
    Application of physical contact
        By feel
        By sound
        By visual means
        With training aids
        Co-ordinated effort

2.3   **Handling skills**
    Dexterity
    Communication
    Anticipation
    Adaptability
    Observation
    Motivation
    Assertiveness

2.4   **Use of timing and owner reactions**
    Reactive timing
    Pleasant approach
    Unpleasant approach

2.5   **Completion of exercise/element**
    Owner's application
    Dog's response – attitude

3. Conclusion

Objective understood by the dog
Probability of consistency and reliability
Linked to Structured Sequence of training
Any side effects   GOOD / BAD   on –
(a) Future training
(b) Other exercises
(c) Safety considerations

Activity breakdown

The art of training is in the attention to detail and sometimes one of the individual details can become lost. This happens when an experienced owner is training a new dog and some of the features of early training with the previous dog have become lost because of habit. The owner had forgotten some of the techniques he had applied in years gone by. This also happens with instructors when little, but important, items of knowledge have disappeared through the repetitive nature of training other owners.

It would be very tedious and impractical to carry out a task analysis on every element of every exercise, but the ability to carry out such an analysis is very useful.

ACTIVITY BREAKDOWN

EXERCISE: TO SIT AND STAY

TASK

To have the dog sit promptly and attentively at the owner's left side. Also to remain sitting.

STANDARD

To achieve an instant response without undue resistance from the dog.

EQUIPMENT

Lead – approx four feet in length.
Material – optional, but comfortable to handle.
(Because of owner discomfort chain leads are considered to be unsuitable)
Collar – Adjustable comi-collar
Traditional buckle style
Collar materials can vary, but should be pliable for comfort.

Method	Key Points
1. Preparation Have dog on collar and lead.	Ensure that collar is suitably adjusted and positioned half way up the dog's neck
2. Preparing owner Lead handling – RIGHT HAND – Loop of lead to be over thumb and held in clenched fist facing in and down. Excess lead also to be held in right hand. LEFT HAND – Working with the lead as near as possible to the clip end (attached to the collar) hold or allow to pass loosely through the clenched hand which is again facing in and down. Lead length between left hand and dog to be just sufficient to prevent it from being taut when dog is close to owner's left side. ARM POSITIONS – Both arms should be extended straight and down with hands approximately in front of their respective legs.	Owner to be physically and mentally prepared to act
3. Preparing dog Owner to create a highly attentive attitude within the dog and have him standing at the owner's left side.	Ensure that the dog is attentive and aware of the activity and will follow through without becoming over excited
4. Generating the dog's attention Owner to apply the dog's name in a manner that will gain the dog's attention. At the same time (if necessary), to tighten the lead sharply with a twist of the left hand, and with just sufficient force to ensure a positive canine reaction.	Owner movements along wth verbal inducements to be synchronised for an immediate canine response
5. Right arm movement Immediately follow up the previous step (4). While maintaining lead loop holding	This action must be an immediate continuation of the previous procedure. The

Method	Key Points
over the right thumb, drop the excess lead from the right hand, cross the right arm over to hold the lead as close to the collar as possible.	right hand will now control the dog's head and the forequarter body movement.
6. Left arm movement Continuous follow through from (5) owner to release lead from left hand and move it to the left side of the dog's croup (groin). Owner to bend and twist his own body along with bent knees while pushing the dog round and to the right so that the dog is manoeuvred into a sit position. At the same time the dog's head is held as close as possible to the owner's left side by means of a tight lead in the right hand.	Again, this movement is an immediate continuation of (6). Owner movements and verbal activities to be synchronised.
7. Release of both hands Release the tension with both hands while giving praise for maintaining the sit position. Owner to be prepared for the dog to think of changing position, tension with both hands can then be immediately reapplied. Verbal instructions to STAY may be required at this juncture. *Note:* Action to prevent canine movement is essential rather than waiting until the dog changes position.	At this stage, the owner must be prepared to react in a manner that will prevent the dog from changing position. Owner's responses to be fully synchronised.
8. Owner regains upright position As the owner praises the dog for staying and instructs him to remain sitting the owner regains the upright and forward facing position. Owner returns hands and lead holding to the earlier item 2 Preparing owner.	During this procedure, the dog may attempt to move and the owner must return to the sequence from item 5 Right arm movement.

Problem identification and analysis

It is the existence of and solutions to training problems that creates the knowledge and experience that is required to prevent the recurrence of these or similar problems. It is the knowledge gained from these problems that helps in the adoption of training methods and programmes to suit specific requirements. This approach has been formulated to give a greater understanding of the basic causes of the various training and consequently behaviour management problems which are regularly encountered.

There are many ways of training a dog, some methods are good and others invite problems. Some owners understand the good methods and execute them in a satisfactory manner while other owners can ruin good sensible methods by a lack of understanding, or an inability to adapt the methods to suit their dogs.

To help analyse the source of a problem and also the stage to start retraining, we should utilise the six basic exercises with handling techniques and stages of training as described in Chapter 13.

FAULT ANALYSIS

A dog's failure to carry out an instruction in a satisfactory manner can be due to a variety of reasons. However, the cause of the failure must be properly analysed and a suitable change of training be applied before an improvement can be attained.

Any Fault Analysis is, therefore, based on the owner's approach to training although one must look initially at the effects of that training – the dog's failure to comply in a satisfactory manner. To analyse a particular fault, one has to consider:

(a) The nature of the fault.
(b) The dog's attitude or frame of mind at the time of failure to comply.
(c) The owner's techniques and mental approach that must be considered to be the cause of the failure.

The nature of the fault may tell a lot, but it is generally the dog's attitude or frame of mind that leads one back to the source of the problem – the owner's techniques or his mental approach to training.

To illustrate this point: If a dog fails to come back to the owner when called, the dog's attitude can tell us a great deal. Does the dog come back and dance round out of the owner's reach because he usually tries to catch his dog? Does the dog just go his own way and ignore his owner because the measure of control is non-existent? Or does the dog stay out of reach because experience has taught him that his owner has shown great displeasure in the past?

An analysis of the owner's techniques and mental approach is also very important, if the reason for failure is to be determined a constructive approach is to be applied to eliminating the fault, or to the prevention of others. It must be necessary to assess the dog's attitude of mind to determine the basis of the owner's failings; the most common can be listed as:

The Dog's Attitude

General note – The various attitudes can be related to situations during training sessions or the management of normal domestic situations.

(a) Uncontrolled Excitement This is generally exhibited by the dog jumping, barking or both in a manner which cannot be controlled by the owner. Although some dogs, especially youngsters, are prone to exhibit such behaviour, excessive praise, for these dogs, can encourage this unwanted conduct. Positive handling with a fair degree of consideration is required to achieve a reasonable measure of control at times when a serious approach is required.

(b) Anticipation Although this is a sign of keenness that should be cultivated and encouraged in the earlier and intermediate stages of training for some exercises, it must be finally brought under full control. This condition should not be confused with uncontrolled excitement.

(c) Inattention A very common situation and can normally be classed as a 'Conflict of Interests' – the dog's interests against those of the owner, where some interesting distraction is having greater effect on the dog than the owner's measure of control in the prevailing situation.

(d) Boredom This is another form of inattention, but more serious, and usually results in the dog making excuses for not complying with the owner's requirements. The most common excuse is to sit and scratch during an exercise, some dogs will even attend to their toilet requirements at such a time when they know that this time wasting activity will go unchecked.

(e) Sluggish Or a slow canine attitude when executing any part of an exercise indicates a complete lack of inattention or boredom. A critical analysis of the owner is required to determine the cause of such a canine attitude.

(f) Defiance May well be due to an independent streak in the dog's character that has not been effectively controlled. On the other hand, an overbearing or unreasonable attitude from the owner may have been the major contribution.

(g) Confusion A dog in a confused state of mind can find the simplest task beyond his reach. Some dogs have a very low threshold to confusion but more owners have an uncanny knack of causing a confused state of mind.

(h) Anxiety or Fear A situation which causes anxiety in a strong willed dog will cause fear in a dog with a limited strength of character. Either situation can cause a confused state of mind, an 'opting out' situation or the type of performance which detracts from the pleasure of dog training.

(i) Failure to Understand Or a misinterpretation of an instruction can be due to so many different causes but may well be mistaken for an act of defiance, simple inattention or may well result in confusion, anxiety or fear.

These canine reactions are normally due to training or handling faults. Extenuating circumstances outside the control of the owner can cause the occasional problem but owners who seem to be 'accident prone' with continual excuses of 'extenuating circumstances' should be extra critical of their own approach. This will ensure that they become fully aware of their own inadequacies.

We all have our weaknesses and improvements can only be made by recognising and working on these weaknesses.

The principle training and handling faults can now be examined and must be accepted by owners as a form of Self Analysis.

1. Owner's Authority This is not an easy factor to regulate and incorrect application is the source of many problems. Although full authority over a dog's activities must be maintained it should always be tempered with consideration and be applied in a manner that will create the desired response. An overbearing approach, especially when it is habitually applied, will certainly create major problems. Defiance, confusion and fear will be high on the list of canine reactions. A lack of authority will certainly be taken by the dog as a weakness in his human partner and this will lead to inattention at the best and complete defiance at its worst.

2. Praise and Punishment The timing and extent of praise to be given cannot be stressed too strongly and should be applied in a manner which will suit the circumstances. Punishment is a non-starter and should never be considered. Remember a dog will respond according to the pleasant or unpleasant situations during the training of an exercise. These pleasant or unpleasant experiences should be manipulated, varied and controlled by the owner to suit the situation. The incorrect application can induce any of the canine reactions from uncontrolled excitement through fear to a complete failure to understand a simple instruction.

3. Amount of Training Excessive training can cause untold problems and is usually due to misplaced enthusiasm on the part of the owner. This can be divided into two broad categories:

(i)　　Each training session being too long and intense.
(ii)　　Too many training sessions within a given period of time, or a combination of both.

To limit the variety of work within training sessions, especially when they are lengthy and intensive, can have a detrimental effect on a dog's performance. Canine and human boredom or inattention can also result from an owner's inability to make training sessions interesting.

The continual repeating of an exercise or the stage of training can cause a very confused canine mind with all its side effects, such as defiance, anxiety or fear. To some dogs, two runs through an exercise or stage are quite sufficient before they lose their edge and, unless a means can be found to maintain a keen interest, serious consideration must be given to curtailing the repeats.

Insufficient training is more likely to be based on a shortage of actual training sessions. Under these circumstances the owner must not expect the dog to maintain the standard of the previous session without an introductory build up.

4. Owner Reaction Many adverse situations become a real problem because the owner failed to recognise the first signs. It must also be considered that a single adverse response, once repeated, is likely to become a habit.

Over-reaction to a fault can cause a confused canine mind with apparent defiance or fear creating failures of greater magnitude than the original problem. One well-known saying that can be heard within certain training circles is that an owner 'sorted his dog out' and an analysis of this action generally reveals a damaged and deteriorating working relationship between dog and owner. Failing to react to a fault will certainly create a changing role in leadership with the owner playing second fiddle to his dog.

5. Stage in Training A proper and flexible programme for training is most important. The failure to include any single stage in progression, to apply an unsuitable sequence of stages, or to fail to consolidate at certain stages can cause quite a variety of problems. To create too big a step between one consolidating stage and another is to disconnect the link between the dog's experience to date and that of tomorrow and will no doubt, cause a failure to understand the owner's requirements,

6. A Combination of Fault Causes Faults are often due to more than one human failure and the resultant canine behaviour can be due to an interaction of a number of handling or training faults.

Care, with an honest assessment, should be made of every handling strength and weakness, also of the appropriate training procedure to determine the root causes of a problem and also the approach required to counteract any apparent weaknesses.

Fault correction

Whenever the cause of a fault has been properly analysed the approach to correction generally becomes self-evident. It must be appreciated that the longer the faulty handling has created an undesirable behaviour the longer it is likely to take to cure the ill.

There are occasions when fast and sharp methods can be applied for correction, but even in these cases, time, a watchful eye and a continued change in approach is required to ensure continuation of a satisfactory performance.

THE APPROACH TO FAULT ANALYSIS

1. Define the problem.
2. Note the exercises affected.
3. Define the handling technique being applied.
4. Note the training stage where the handling technique is creating the fault.
5. Determine the dog's attitude under the listing A to J on page 163.
6. Note the owner's attitude and approach to the appropriate handling technique that is causing the undesirable canine attitude; refer to Items 1 to 6, listed on pages 164-5.
7. Apply the necessary changes to the owner's attitude or handling technique at the appropriate stage in the training routine, rebuild on a more successful approach.

Planning training sessions can make a big difference to most instructors. There are so many factors to be considered that it is easy to overlook something. It is generally, at the stage of writing the details down that there is a realisation that something is amiss. Such record of details also helps to create consistency or the need to make changes from one course to the other. The following is just an example for the first session within such a plan.

SESSION INSTRUCTIONAL PLAN

Training Session – One   Duration one and a half hours
Equipment – Collar, lead.

SESSION and TECHNIQUES

INTRODUCTION
a) Welcome students, registration, and introduction.
b) Course objectives.
c) Distribute course programme and discuss   Talk
   development of training exercises.
d) Note and discuss problems.   Question and answer

ATTENTION GENERATING
   Describe-Demonstrate-Instruct
a) Lead handling.   Talk – Practical
b) Response to call of name.   All dogs and individually
c) Backward movement,
   Repeat as required   Question and answer

SIT AND STAY

Describe-Demonstrate Instruct	Talk - Practical
a) Immediate Sit – Physical method.	All dogs together
b) Stand straddled with sit and stay.	All dogs together
Repeat As required	Question and answer

Instructor to discuss the progress to date with observations and comments from both owners and instructor.

Being the first session of a course, it is important that owners and dogs are put at ease. They should feel that they are being treated as individuals – important individuals. The more instructors know, the easier it becomes to forget the simple and natural things that come to us. When carrying out a handling procedure or a technique there are very important activities, which, if not described or demonstrated to the owner, will leave him uncertain of the instruction.

With complete beginners in the world of computers, these people just had to look at the earlier instruction books to realise the seemingly small, but important instructions were missing. With this in mind, it is worth considering the application of the Activity Breakdown technique described earlier in this chapter.

Chapter 16

UNDERSTANDING COMMITMENT AND SPECIAL NEEDS

Commitment

I would like to re-enforce some earlier views and emphasise the importance of the subject of personal commitment and direct involvement of the owner to achieve an acceptable behaviour level or a specific standard in training for their dogs, be it for domestic, competitive or professional purposes.

Over the years, I have studied the commitment of owners when they are training their dogs, or when I have been attending to elementary problems and often found owner commitment to be the principal subject of my concern. It is important that dog owners appreciate that they can benefit greatly from the type of assistance that will meet their particular requirements.

Studying people for the purpose of improving training methods and handling techniques is just as important as studying their dogs. It is the owner who creates the end product – an obedient dog or a disobedient one, a worthy competitor or an 'also ran', an effective professional or a liability. When working to create a canine reaction, commitment is important. We are expecting full concentration from the dog when it is requested and he deserves the same concentration from the person creating that reaction.

Unfortunately, full commitment from the owner is not always forthcoming during training and today's tendency to use titbits, toys or some other gadget as a training aid often becomes a substitute for full commitment. I am not condemning the use of such training aids, I make use of them myself, but observation has taught me that many instructors and behaviourists are too dependent on the use of these aids when assisting or directing a dog owner in the use of conditioning techniques.

Training a dog to perform a task, or to eradicating an undesirable action, is a form of positive conditioning for the desired response. It is easier to be inclusive of both situations by describing a procedure as one of conditioning the dog's action or reaction.

Over the years, I have watched the form of owner commitment change. My own activities have changed. During the 1950s when I entered the scene of dog training, depth of commitment from the owner was much less reliant on titbits, toys and the like, than it is today. Unfortunately, that level of commitment in a number of cases did create a harsher and, at the time, a more brutal approach from a section of the training fraternity.

Although I was brought up in the branch of a club where harsh treatment was not an option, there were a number of clubs where the desire for success would bring out the worst, and not the best, in a proportion of owners. I recall one situation where a club instructor took a German Shepherd from his owner to demonstrate how she should be applying total commitment with her dog. After a few minutes of strict compulsion the dog managed to break free, ran out of the hall and was lost for three months before he found his way home – with shotgun pellets in his thick coat.

My first German Shepherd, Quest, worked well in both Working trials and Obedience. He became a Working Trials Champion, but we were not quite committed enough to win an Obedience 'ticket'. I was advised by a particular section of competitors to keep Quest in a kennel when he was not being exercised or trained and this exclusion from my company for such periods would result in greater commitment from him. However, I saw no sense in having a canine companion in isolation for the sake of greater success in a field of competition.

The change to the conditions that prevail today is now so dramatic that titbits, toys and gadgets have taken the desired personal commitment out of conditioning for a cooperative canine response. The problem is that when inappropriate use of training aids is applied to generate canine attention this does not prepare the dog, or the owner, for situations when these aids are not at hand. There are so many occasions in real life when a training aid is not immediately available when instant action is a necessity. The training aid may be in a pocket or a belly bag and, by the time the aid is available for application, it is too late. There are also many situations when a dog is distracted to the degree that these training aids are of no practical value.

This is where a particular expression of mine comes to mind 'A dog will always respond to an inducement that is strong enough to counter his immediate desires'. When properly applied, a dog will always appreciate commitment from an owner and this will also enhance the companionship.

SPECIAL NEEDS FOR DOGS

We hear and read often enough about children with special needs, and of some of the causes. We could probably look at dogs and children and find that many of the problems have similar root causes. As a means of comparison, I would like to try and define the root causes with children to help understand the problems with dogs, but my layman's understanding of child delinquency is just not enough to become involved in such a specialised subject. However, when I watch television programmes on the handling of child delinquents I find that the experts are using methods I have been applying for many years in the prevention and correction of canine training or behavioural situations. The readers, at this time, may wish to make their own judgements on any similarities or differences between the causes and the remedies when dealing with children or with dogs.

What do we mean when we think about dogs with special needs? It could be said that any dog would come into this category, if it is a problem to his owner or considered to be so by members of the community. However, because of the divergence of magnitudes and causes, there is a variance in needs from one dog to another.

When do we consider that a dog comes into the category of special needs? I can only give my own assessment of that situation. I believe it is when a dog becomes a problem to his owner or any reasonable member of the community. A dog that does not respond to:

(a) The owner's own approach to correcting an undesirable situation through basic training,
(b) The similar approach being given by an outside body (this could be the standard approach at a dog training class). Or
(c) Dogs with well-balanced characters and are given advanced training for the enjoyment of both owner and dog, or for distinctive and professional purposes can also be classed as specialist cases – and for honourable reasons.

It is unfortunate some owners do not appreciate that the behaviour of their dogs bring them into the special needs category, that they do need some form of conditioning or training beyond the norm to eliminate or reduce the effect of their canine problems. It will therefore be recognised that it is usually the owner's failure to appreciate there is a real problem that is the source of the undesirable situation and there is a need for special attention.

Many owners realise there is a problem and, quite rightly, they take their dogs along to a training class. They are sensible about it; most listen and do their best.

Some dogs are not suited to the homes they go into. The owners are too weak or lacking in understanding. It can be said that some breeds are not suited to a relatively inactive domestic environment. I dislike seeming to pick on particular breeds when I am writing, but I must give a few illustrations.

The Springer spaniel has been bred as a working dog, to flush out and work along with the gun. At a seminar I attended some time ago, the breeding and puppy manager for the Metropolitan Police told us that this breed was the second largest in numbers serving that organisation. He also said that these Springers did not have an 'off' switch. They were little busy bodies and thrived on the work they did. As drug or explosive dogs, these dogs are hard to beat.

Collies were also bred to work. They seemed to be fitted with everlasting batteries – they never run down. Put some of them into a domestic environment with nothing to occupy their minds and not a sheep in sight and trouble can be round the corner. Worse still, with sheep round the corner and no control over the dog there is bigger trouble.

My own breed, the German Shepherd, with his size and natural guarding ability, must be conditioned to respect the rights of others round him. For those breeds and many more, special needs can mean training in a constructive manner to utilise their outstanding abilities. The Springer spaniel working for his job intended, or sniffing for drugs or explosives will never think of, or have the time to get into trouble. The Border collie comes into the same category and, although it is unlikely that a German Shepherd will be seen working sheep in the UK they are the most suited for police work. Those are all professional duties, but there are so many other outlets for dogs of all kinds, and not necessarily pure bred animals.

Keeping a dog's mind active for the owner's pleasure can take many forms. By playing with their dogs in a controllable manner, so many owners have avoided problems. Taking up one of the more advanced training outlets at the various clubs can turn simple ownership into one of an enjoyable partnership. Gun dog training is an obvious for the owners of suitable breeds. Agility and flyball are now a great pastime for so many pet dog owners and these activities can keep many a dog out of trouble. Obedience and Working trials have a following of dedicated pet dog owners who take their training very seriously. Dancing to music with a dog has now become a very popular activity. When we see the enjoyment Mary Rae and her dogs get out of this activity during her performance at Crufts, we can realise that training classes for this purpose would be very enjoyable. Every dog and his activities deserves to be considered as special in some way and by somebody.

THE REVERSING OF ROLES

During the various aspects already discussed within the partnership between dog and owner it will be obvious that the owner plays a leading role within that relationship with the dog as the junior partner. Although this is a natural partnership, it can only be successful with consideration and thought to develop a full understanding of each other. The more successful it becomes the more it appears to be a partnership of equal proportions. The more advanced the training, the more dependent the owner and dog become on the contributions from each other.

In certain circumstances, the dog is purposely trained or conditioned to become the senior or leading partner. This generally takes place when the dog is much more capable than man when carrying out the function in specific circumstances. A few of these circumstances come to mind and they can all be termed as professional activities, although some can be trained and practiced by parties considered to be non-professional personnel.

A keen dog starting a training track.

These activities are usually based on the dog's scenting ability or the protective genes that run through the dog's inherited makeup. Tracking, property searching, including drugs and explosives along with mountain rescue all require the finely tuned scenting ability of so many breeds and cross breeds. Criminal work, security and the like require dogs with courage and the ability to be controlled. In all such occasions with scenting or protection work the dog is taught to think and act in a manner that comes through from his most primitive instincts. He is taught to take charge of the situation with his owner (or professional handler) giving the backing and confidence that may be required.

Although the partnership responsibilities will change between dog and owner as situations change, it is the manner in which the dogs have been guided in training that determines the success and respect dogs and owners have for each other.

One situation where dogs are trained to become the senior partner has not been included in the above is that of working for the blind. It is not the dog's scenting power, or his protective (as in criminal work) nature that controls the dog's activities. It may well be the dog's loyalty that is the major factor.

It does take special dogs and specialised training to create a canine senior partner in that field of work and the expression of 'Special needs' expands well beyond the accepted terminology of 'canine delinquency'.

Author (blindfolded) with Seeing Eye dog and trainer negotiating the traffic in Morristown, New Jersey.

INDEX